CULT ROCK
POSTERS 1972-1982

Pop art borrowed from real pop and we're taking it back again.
Pete Townshend, 1966

CULT ROCK POSTERS 1972-1982

A HISTORY
FROM BOYS IN DRAG TO BUFFALO GALS

ROGER CRIMLIS &
ALWYN W TURNER

Aurum

First published 2006 by Aurum Press Limited,
25 Bedford Avenue,
London WC1B 3AT

All images taken from the authors' personal poster collection. Photography by
Fernando Mañoso-Borgas and Jon Meade.

A catalogue record for this book is available from the British Library.

ISBN-10 1 84513 129 0
ISBN-13 978 1 84513 129 6

1 3 5 7 9 10 8 6 4 2
2006 2008 2010 2009 2007

Design by Ghost
Printed and bound in China

CONTENTS

PLEASE ALLOW ME TO INTRODUCE MYSELF...

In rock & roll mythology the 1960s ended in the mud of the Altamont speedway track, California on 6 December 1969, as a black man named Meredith Hunter lay bleeding to death from the knife wounds inflicted by white Hell's Angels. The fact that a few feet away the Rolling Stones were on stage swaggering their way through 'Under My Thumb', the most cocky anthem of swinging London, only added to the symbolism of the moment. The arrogant optimism of the mid-'60s came crashing up against the outlaw fringe of the counter-culture – irresponsible force meeting bone-headed object – and brought the decade to a depressing and disreputable end.

Elsewhere, seemingly in another universe, the Archies were at #1 in the British singles chart with their bubblegum classic 'Sugar Sugar'. This was a band two counter-revolutions away from the '60s dream. For pop fans upset by the Beatles' desire to be mystics rather than moptops, American TV had invented the Monkees. Then, for an entertainment industry upset by Mike Nesmith's desire to be a musician rather than a puppet, American TV invented the Archies, a group that not only didn't play on their own records, but didn't even exist: they were the cartoon heroes of an animated show – from yogis to Yogi Bear in two easy steps. Without breaking cartoon sweat, the Archies managed to sell six million copies of 'Sugar Sugar' to score the biggest international hit of the year.

The gap that had opened between rock and pop had never been wider. Five years earlier there had been no distinction made between the two; now it seemed barely believable that they came from the same tradition. But they had one thing in common: they were both in crisis.

And then things got worse.

For rock, the twelve months that followed Altamont proved a traumatic and agonizing hangover: the Beatles split, the Stones went into temporary retirement and the deaths of Jimi Hendrix and Janis Joplin were announced, to be followed a few months later by Jim Morrison. For pop meanwhile, the *reductio ad absurdum* of 'Sugar Sugar' was followed to #1 by the kitsch Victoriana of Rolf Harris's 'Two Little Boys', the record that the British public chose to take them into the brave new decade of the '70s.

The effect of this separation of rock and pop was everywhere evident in 1970, nowhere more so than when it came to the question of singles. In January of that year, Pink Floyd announced that they would never release another single – a position they maintained for almost the entire decade until they finally relented to score the last #1 of the '70s with 'Another Brick In The Wall' – and their stance was not unusual. Of the UK's twenty best-selling albums in 1970, half were accounted for by British acts: Led Zeppelin, the Beatles, Paul McCartney, Deep Purple, the Moody Blues, Black Sabbath, the Rolling Stones and Free. Yet between them these artists produced just five singles that made the top 50 that year: 'Let It Be', 'Black Night', 'Question', 'Paranoid' and 'All Right Now'. As an art form, the three-minute 7-inch seemed to be dying of neglect.

On the one hand there were serious musicians keen to get their heads together in the country, reluctant to admit that they were now, or ever had been, members of the industry of human happiness, and determined – in the case of Led Zeppelin – never to give an interview nor to appear on television, self-promotion being too vulgar for artists of their stature. On the other hand, there was a singles chart that, denied access to the brightest talent of a new generation, had to find its material in the ranks of professional songwriters employing professional musicians to manufacture a suitably professional product. So shameless and seamless had British pop become, so dependent on studio-players, that early in 1970 session-singer Tony Burrows made three appearances on a single episode of *Top of the Pops* as a member of what purported to be three different bands. And even that didn't tell the whole story: at the time he had four singles in the top 20, under the names of Brotherhood of Man, White Plains, Edison Lighthouse and the Pipkins.

The effect on both rock and pop was a complete loss of interest in image. Bands from the denimocracy played the college circuit trying to look as much like their audience as possible in case anyone accused them of being frivolous; studio-bound pop musicians played *Top of the Pops* trying to look as anonymous as possible in case anyone recognized them from last week's band. Whether you liked the blues-rock of Ten Years After or the pure froth of Christie's #1 hit 'Yellow River', you could be sure of this:

You really didn't want their picture on your wall.

1 DRIVING ME BACKWARDS

He and John had a long discussion about what I should be called. We waded through such names as Saul Lust, Norman Passion, Dan Satan, Rummy Duggan, Dan de Lion (ouch!), Toby Jugg, Mark Venus.
Royston Ellis, *Myself For Fame* (Consul, London, 1964)

The wall was something of a shrine, a real work of art, dedicated to the mods, the fashions, the music, the scooters. I'd taken most of the pictures from the New Musical Express, Titbits and Reveille.
Alan Fletcher, *Quadrophenia* (Corgi, London, 1979)

If some kid was going to buy a poster of me and put it on their wall, then I wanted it to be a fantasy figure of the calibre they'd never meet on the bus going to school. Gary Glitter had to be a fictional character as far removed from their reality as possible.
Gary Glitter, *Leader* (Ebury, London, 1991)

'**G**lam rock,' John Lennon once pointed out, 'is just rock & roll with lipstick on.' Which didn't really do justice to the lipstick. Because lipstick was essentially what the best of 1970s rock was all about, from the Pierre Laroche-applied gloss of David Bowie and the black void of Lou Reed, through the ironic scarlet-lipped starlets Debbie Harry and Siouxsie, to the painted pout of Adam Ant. The lipstick killers of the '70s deliberately turned their backs on the legacy of the late '60s, replacing authenticity with artifice, careful craftsmanship with carefree playfulness and dressing down with dressing up. Appearances were, if not everything, then at least an integral part of everything. Everything that mattered.

It began in the early summer of 1972 when glam broke through as a major force in the British charts. Initially seen by the high-minded end of the music establishment as a novelty of limited appeal and dubious merit, this strange new genre nonetheless announced the arrival of a visually literate strand in rock that was to set the agenda for the next decade and beyond. Both glam and punk – the continuation of glam by other means – self-consciously set standards that reasserted the primacy of style and image in popular culture.

In an era when promo-films scarcely existed, when rock on TV was a strictly rationed affair and when the first glossy music magazine had yet to be printed, the poster was one of the few means available of conveying that image to fans and potential fans. 'Did you hang my picture on your wall?' Gary Glitter demanded in his 1973 hit 'Hello, Hello, I'm Back Again', and both he and his audience knew it was a rhetorical question. Posters were a shorthand declaration of intent, asserting allegiances, fuelling fantasies and letting friends know where one stood in the grand scheme of rock & roll. Whether they were record shop displays, fly-posters, gig promotions, magazine centrefolds or commercial cash-ins available from Woolworths, posters were everywhere. And they were as crucial to the artists as they were to the fans.

The posters featured in this book are predominantly of musicians from an artistic tradition in British and American rock that found new expression in the 1970s. Mostly photographic, mostly focused on imagery of the band, they aim to communicate a direct and simple message. If there is a single theme, then it is one of attitude and approach: the

TYRANNOSAURUS REX

Tyrannosaurus Rex (1969)
A somewhat literal interpretation of the band's name, this was issued by Blue Thumb, the independent label that released Bolan's early records in the States. Dating from pre-glam, pre-stardom days, this is perhaps the smallest image of Bolan ever seen on a poster. The typeface (Broadway) is an unusually early example of the kind of art deco styling that would become associated with T. Rex in the '70s; the record sleeves from the period were still using art nouveau lettering.

Photography & design Tom Wilkes (Blue Thumb) 20 x 32 inches, 81 x 51cm

idea that, as epitomized by the Ramones, every aspect of a performer's work should be a coherent, unified whole. 'I deliver a complete package,' Bryan Ferry explained early on in Roxy Music's career; 'something not only has to sound good, but also has to feel good and look good.' Detail was everything: theoretically it should have been possible to take a sample from Bowie's Yakamoto-designed knitted body-stocking and, from the cultural DNA, recreate the entirety of Ziggy Stardust. Or the spirit of punk from the ripped graphics in a Jamie Reid poster for the Sex Pistols.

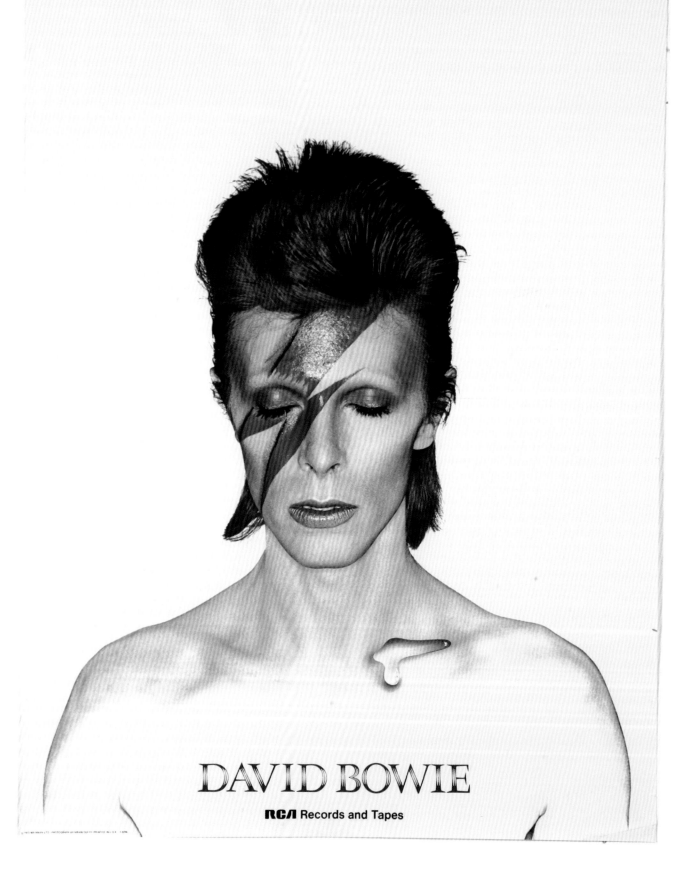

DAVID BOWIE

As a member of the New York band Television, Richard Hell designed their early gig posters – simple black and white printed A4 sheets that bore a photo, the names both of the group and of its members, and little more. 'The main idea was not to elaborate,' he reflects, 'but to let the facts speak for themselves, because the facts were strong and seductive.'

Which allows for a subtle shift in what constituted 'facts', since two of the four band members were identified by assumed names: Tom Verlaine and Hell himself.

And names were important. In the '60s pseudonyms had hardly existed in mainstream rock. Of the members of the British bands that dominated that decade only two had assumed new names, and one of those was the decidedly unglamorous sounding Bill Wyman. (The other was Ringo Starr, who was the first to welcome glam, directing Marc Bolan's film *Born to Boogie*.) But in the '70s the adoption of stage names became virtually the norm, from David Bowie and Alvin Stardust to Johnny Rotten and Joe Strummer, and back again to Adam Ant and Steve Strange. Even the most straight sounding turned out to be an alter-ego: Steve Harley, for example, had been born Steven Nice. Few went to the lengths of Gary Glitter, who in January 1973 staged a mock funeral for his previous incarnation as Paul Raven, but throughout the period there was a tendency towards reinvention, a feeling that the creation of a public persona was part of the job description for a putative rock & roll star.

There was a precedent for such artifice, and it went back to the pre-Beatles British music scene, to the very infancy of rock & roll, and particularly to the stable of artists managed by Larry Parnes: Tommy Steele, Marty Wilde, Billy Fury, Vince Eager, Duffy Power, Georgie Fame and all the others. During the '60s this novelty nomenclature fell out of favour, as rock music sought to establish its grown-up credentials, but by the end of the decade the scent of revival was in the air, and the naivety and purity of the early days was beginning to look ever more appealing.

This rock & roll revival, beginning in 1969, is the great unacknowledged subtext of the '70s. Multi-artist gigs at Toronto and Madison Square Garden in the autumn of that year, featuring first-generation rockers, followed on from Sha Na Na's appearance at Woodstock, while the hottest American band were Creedence Clearwater Revival (the clue was in the third word of their name). The Beatles, recognizing the new mood, included 'One After 909' on *Let It Be* (1970), a song they had written back in 1960, and John Lennon made his return to the live stage at Toronto, alongside Chuck Berry, Jerry Lee Lewis and Little Richard.

In Britain the revival was heralded by Dave Edmunds' 1970 cover of the Smiley Lewis song 'I Hear You Knocking', which reached #1, and in 1972 the live spectacular arrived with the first ever rock gig at Wembley Stadium. Significantly, the now standard line-up of veterans on that occasion was joined by a sprinkling of those who were to take the music forwards: proto-punks the MC5 and Dr

David Bowie – *Aladdin Sane* (1973)
The most enduring of Bowie's '70s images was photographed by Brian Duffy with make-up by Pierre Laroche. This American poster changed the colouring of the text and omitted the name of the album, instead using the image as a general promotion of the artist. The framing of the image within the poster is strikingly eccentric.

Photography & album design Brian Duffy & Celia Philo (MainMan/RCA Records & Tapes) 24 x 36 inches, 91 x 61cm

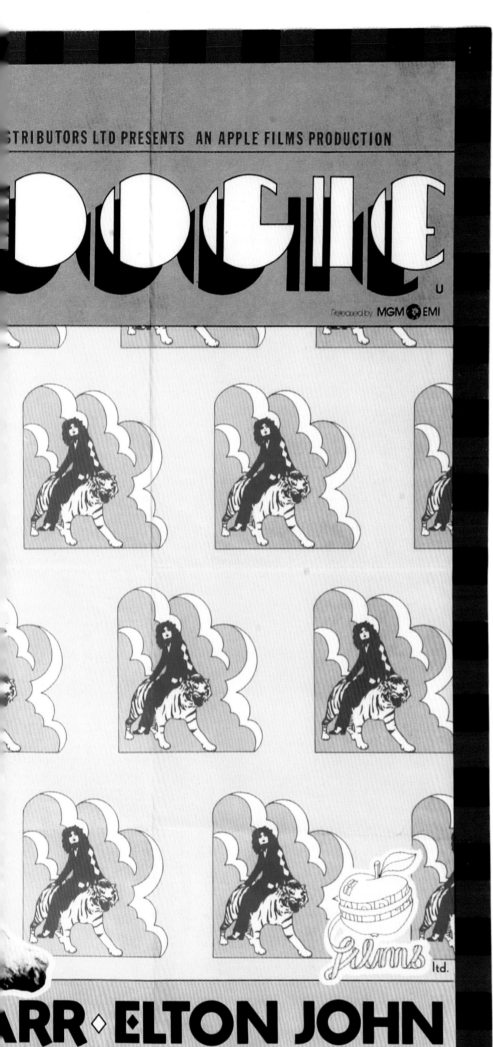

Left

Born To Boogie (1972)

T. Rex's concert movie *Born to Boogie* was released by Apple Films in December 1972 with a poster that tapped into the growing art deco revival. The typeface and the repeated motif deliberately referred back to the era when Hollywood was enjoying its glory days, while the exclusive focus on Bolan – both pictorially and in his solo billing – emphasized his star status above the music.

Keith Morris (1938–2005) was the official photographer for the shooting of the movie, having known Bolan since the days of the '60s counter-culture. Born in London in 1938, he contributed to *IT*, *Oz* and *Time Out* and continued to shoot rock acts through the '70s.

Photography Keith Morris (Apple Films/EMI; printed by WE Berry, Bradford) 30 x 40 inches, 115 x 76cm

15

Feelgood (the latter serving as backing band for former teen idol Heinz), and the glam acts Wizzard and Gary Glitter. The same year saw the opening off, and very soon on, Broadway of the musical *Grease*, to be followed in 1973 by the movies *American Graffiti* and *That'll Be The Day* (a kind of *Anglian Graffiti*) and in 1974 by *Happy Days* on TV.

High-concept glam rockers also paid their dues to this cultural current, with Bowie taking revival band Fumble out on tour as support act (and recording Chuck Berry's 'Round and Round'), and Eno encoring on his 1974 tour with a version of Neil Sedaka's 'I Go Ape'. Indeed the drive backwards was such that it even infected the rarefied world of subsidized drama in Britain. David Hare's play *Teeth 'n' Smiles* was first staged in 1975, but was set in the dying days of the '60s and concerned a band falling apart at the seams, causing their manager to recall the glory years: 'It'll never get better than 1956. Tat. Utter tat. But inspired. The obvious repeated many times. Simple things said well. Then along came those boys who could really play. They spoilt it of course. Ruined it.' He was talking about the time that he first met a singer named Tony Torrent, played in the first production by Heinz, who'd made it all the way from Wembley to the Royal Court Theatre.

This resurgence of interest in old-school rock & roll carried with it a sense of completion, an implicit assumption that the music had reached a sufficient maturity to allow it to look back. Even more powerful, however, was a feeling of failure. 'People weren't as obsessed in the '60s with holding on to the past,' remembers underground entrepreneur and record producer Joe Boyd. 'There wasn't an obsession with the past because one was very optimistic about the present and the future.' All that was to change.

With the elections of reactionary politicians Richard Nixon as US President in 1968 and Ted Heath as British Prime Minister in 1970 – and with the Manson murders and the violence of Altamont in between – it was becoming apparent that the radical-liberal agenda of the hippie dream had failed to bring about the immediate transformation of society that it had sought. The continuous drive forward, the social progressiveness that was mirrored in the musical experimentations of the Beatles and Bob Dylan, had ground to a halt. The original generation of rock fans, now in their late twenties and early thirties, had itself reached a stage of taking stock and reflection, and a programme of back-to-

basics, driven by a desire to recapture the lost innocence of its youth, was fabulously alluring. Although this yearning was initiated by the '50s revival, it wasn't long before it affected other areas. By the summer of 1971 the British magazine *Record Mirror* was offering its readers a special deal on West Coast psychedelic posters, a set of four available for sixty pence plus fifteen pence p&p: 'Bright, colourful and now a part of history – that's the set of event posters imported straight from San Francisco.' Nostalgia, in short, was fast becoming business. Out of this new mood came glam rock, and if it sometimes seemed primitive, even childish, then that was because it was. Deliberately. This was, in the context of rock music's newly discovered sense of a life-history, a playful retreat to a pre-adult world. It was a licence to make-believe.

Marc Bolan

Above - Left

T. Rex - Autumn Tour (1971)

A double-sided poster that was sold as official merchandise during the 1971 T. Rex tour. By January 1972 copies of this were being offered for mail-order sale exclusively by Cauldron Promotions of London NW6 at a discount price of thirty pence each or two for fifty pence (plus fifteen pence p&p). The advert also carried the warning: 'Please note that the poster is supplied to us folded (although we will dispatch it to you rolled) but the creases can be ironed out if desired.'

20 x 30 inches, 76 x 51cm

Above

Marc Bolan - *Sun* newspaper (1972)

These shots of Bolan were taken during the filming of *Born to Boogie*, and the poster was offered to readers of the *Sun* newspaper in Britain. At the time, the *Sun* was coming back from near-extinction and had its sights set on overtaking the *Daily Mirror* as the biggest-selling daily paper; pop was one of the weapons used in the circulation wars, though this was one of the rare examples where they got it right – *The Sun Annual for Boys* (1973) restricted its pop coverage to Arlo Guthrie, Al Stewart and Gordon Lightfoot.

Photography Keith Morris (the *Sun*) 30 x 40 inches, 115 x 76cm

The first to build a successful career out of the changed times was Marc Bolan. Born Mark Feld, he had been one of the original mods, had strayed into art-rock with the band John's Children, and had made a minor name for himself as a hippy with the acoustic duo Tyrannosaurus Rex, sitting cross-legged on a carpeted stage and singing about elves and unicorns. When he elected to shorten the band's name to the more manageable T. Rex, strap on a Strat and go back to the elemental chord changes that had first made him fall in love with rock & roll, the result was an immediate hit; 'Ride A White Swan' was a twelve-bar boogie that was kept from the UK #1 slot only by Clive Dunn's 1970 Christmas novelty 'Grandad' (written, as it happens, by a man who would be Bolan's last-ever bassist, Herbie Flowers).

T. Rex followed with a pair of #1 singles, 'Hot Love' and 'Get It On', and a #1 album *Electric Warrior*, all cheerfully blending pre-Beatles rock with Dylan-derived surrealistic lyrics and amped-up blues riffs. The band was the story of 1971 in Britain, the first act for years to inspire teen hysteria, and the first attempt to heal the late-'60s rift between rock and pop, bringing integrity to singles and fun to albums. In the process Bolan shed some of his erstwhile counter-cultural followers but showed no sign of remorse, wallowing instead in the warm embrace of his new teenybopper constituency. Even his language in interviews seemed calculated to provoke anger amongst those he was leaving behind, playing on the generational conflict that had dominated the '60s: 'If there is going to be any kind of revolution in pop,' he declared, 'it must come from the young people; if you ignore them you are cutting yourself off from the life-supply of the rock music force.'

With hindsight, Bolan is seen as the man who founded glam, but at the time of his early hits – when no such genre was known to exist – his image was hardly excessive. Although he sprinkled a little glitter on his face, the clothes he was wearing in 1971 at the peak of his success were available at any decent high-street boutique, and looked almost muted next to the outfits favoured by the likes of Mick Jagger, let alone compared to the memory of Jimi Hendrix, Bolan's own favourite point of reference.

Musically, too, his themes were far from original, even at the time of his breakthrough. A series of hits earlier in 1970 – the Kinks' 'Lola', Mungo Jerry's 'In The Summertime' and

Hotlegs' 'Neanderthal Man' – had between them established much of what would come to be known as glam: gender confusion, traditional chord sequences and raw, upfront rhythms respectively. 'Marc said that when "In The Summertime" became such a huge hit, he realized you could have a hit pop song with a twelve-bar,' reflects Mungo Jerry's sideburned singer Ray Dorset. 'Well, people had been doing that for years . . . ' But Bolan had the magic extra ingredient, the lipstick, as it were: he was a self-proclaimed star.

In a world where musos were indistinguishable from fans, Bolan preened like a movie goddess from the golden age. The parallel was not unreasonable. Hollywood in the '30s and '40s had been populated not so much by actors and actresses but by stars, whose job it was to be themselves in a succession of films – no one went to see a movie with Joan Crawford in it; rather, they went to see a Joan Crawford movie, safe in the knowledge that, while the setting, the story and the supporting cast might have changed from the last time round, Crawford herself would remain splendidly and defiantly herself. ('If you want to see the girl next door,' she proclaimed, 'go next door.') This attitude was revived by Bolan. Having achieved the full realization of his artistic vision on 'Hot Love', he simply repeated it on a dozen follow-up singles. There was no development, just a reiteration of style, despite his own protestations: 'I always say each single is different from the last,' he lamented in 1974, 'but everybody says they all sound the same.'

Back in 1899 Sir Hubert Parry – the composer, most famously, of 'Jerusalem' – had defended English folk music against what he saw as the degeneracy of popular songs; there was in folk, he said, 'no sham, no got-up glitter and no vulgarity.' That was precisely what Bolan was offering: sham, glam and vulgarity.

And a grateful nation lapped it up.

Because Bolan's Hollywood-derived notion of stardom was not an isolated incident. It gelled with the mood of the times. As Britain began to enter the come-down from the amphetamine high of the mid-'60s and to head towards recession, the iconography of the Great Depression became ever more popular. Musically the revival may have been

'50s, but elsewhere the London superstore-boutique Biba was offering cut-price Busby Berkeley fantasies to all, while the musicals *Cabaret* and *The Boy Friend* (first staged in 1954 but filmed by Ken Russell in 1971) were celebrating the escapism of the '20s and '30s. The trend can be seen in the poster that announced the launch of Dingwalls, a new venue in Camden Lock, London, and which – entirely inappropriately for the venue – used a still of Rita Hayworth from the 1942 film *You Were Never Lovelier*.

Similarly the standard line trotted out to describe the undeniable visual appeal of an up-and-coming singer-songwriter named David Bowie was that he resembled Lauren Bacall, a claim resting mostly on his image on the 1971 album *Hunky Dory*. In fact, when Main Artery, the design company set up by Bowie's childhood friend, the artist George Underwood, was given the photo to colourize for the sleeve, it was presented as a sepia-tinted duotone picture. Presumably the idea of releasing it in sepia – the standard shorthand for nostalgia – had previously been considered, which would have made the echoes of the Hollywood Highs even more resonant.

Left

David Bowie - Plymouth gig poster (1972)
This poster for a gig on the Ziggy Stardust tour (designed by Jim Corridan, the then brother-in-law of local promoter Greg Vandike) draws on the post-hippy/Lauren Bacall image of *Hunky Dory* period Bowie. The existence of such a dated image indicates how ill-coordinated publicity campaigns were at the time.

Design Jim Corridan (Vandike Organization) 23 x 17.5 inches, 58.5 x 45cm

BOWIE
PINUPS

L.P. RS 1003
Cassette PK 11669
Cartridge P8S

RCA

Previous Page - Left

Dingwalls Dancehall (1973)

'That's how people tried to dress: '40s dresses, wedges, platforms, that hair, the eyebrows,' says Poly Styrene. 'All the groupies, the girls who used to hang out at places like Dingwalls hoping to meet band members, that's what they'd be trying to do. That's what you'd see on TV when you were growing up, all those old Hollywood movies.'

Habitués of Max's Kansas City, home of the art underground in New York, would also have noted the reference on the poster to 'Steaks, Hamburgers, Chick Peas', a nod to Max's slogan: 'Steaks, Lobsters, Chick Peas'.

Photography George Hurrell; design David King (Dingwalls; printed by Plough Press, London) 21.5 x 31 inches, 78.5 x 55cm

Previous Page - Right

David Bowie - *Pinups* (1973)

Pinups was Bowie's tribute to his mod roots and the cover featured a Justin de Villeneuve photograph of him with Twiggy, both made-up with white masks by Pierre Laroche: with Bowie it emphasized the artificiality of his persona even when covering old r&b songs; with Twig the Wonder Kid it covered her tan after a Caribbean holiday. The photo was originally taken for *Vogue* magazine, for whom it was intended as the first double-shot cover, until Bowie requested it for his own use. The poster trimmed both left and right sides and moved the lettering to create a portrait-shaped image.

Photography Justin de Villeneuve (RCA Records & Tapes) 20.5 x 28.5 inches, 72 x 52cm

Left

Alice Cooper – 1972 Calendar (1971)

This calendar came free with the album *Killer*, released in the last months of 1971, and was immediately controversial: parents hated it, schools banned it, MPs denounced it but it was on the walls of the hippest kids in the country for a full twelve months. So, was it intended to provoke controversy? 'Of course!' says Alice. 'Who else was doing anything like that back then? No one!' 'It was a shocking image for that time,' agrees Adam Ant. 'It was pretty horrible. My mum really didn't like it.'

The image of the hanged artist was revived by Eddie & the Hot Rods on their second album, *Life on the Line* (1977), with individual shots of each group member in a noose. Without the make-up and theatrical staging of Alice, it was actually an even more disturbing image, dangerously close to realism: drummer Steve Nicol on the cover looks like a genuine teenage suicide.

Photography Pete Turner (Warner Brothers) 12 x 24 inches, 30.5 x 61cm

While Bolan was reinventing pop in Britain, so Alice Cooper (both the man, born Vincent Furnier, and the group that took his assumed name) were doing the same with rock in the States. At a time when heavy metal, its hour come round at last, was slouching like a rough beast towards Birmingham to be born, Alice instead offered an alternative way forward for hard rock, via the cosmetics counter and the dressing-up box.

Unlike Bolan with his mod/hippy background, the Alice Cooper band came out of the scuzzier end of American punk in the mid-'60s. Previously known as the Earwigs, the Spiders and the Nazz, Alice Cooper released their first two albums on Frank Zappa's Straight label, but – according to Alice himself – were kicked off because their propensity for make-up suggested a sexual ambivalence with which Zappa could not cope. Teaming up instead with producer Bob Ezrin, the band abandoned their avant-garage style in favour of a much more straightforward, commercial brand of guitar rock that produced a debut US hit in 1971 with the anthem 'Eighteen'.

In Britain neither the single nor its accompanying album (*Love It To Death*) made the charts but Alice was still big news. Having dragged himself up from the breadline, he invested his money wisely in producing the most spectacular live show that any had yet attempted in rock & roll. The word soon spread from America that this was something very special and by June 1971 he was holding forth to the British rock press on the revolutionary effect the band had on its followers: 'If a fourteen-year-old boy comes home with make-up on and his father, who wanted him to be a wrestler, hits him in the head with a rock, that's politics. . .'

At this point Alice's appearance was much less malevolent than it was later to become: the painting around his eyes, for example, formed a spider's web rather than the pitch-black hell-holes with which he was to become associated.

But the obsession with make-up and image, the insistence that this had a personal-political dimension, the commitment to riff-hungry rock and the direct appeal to the adolescent music fan – these foolish things tied Alice to Bolan and laid the foundations for the nascent genre of glam.

The influence of the Alice Cooper band on Britain was enormous, if not always admitted. When David Bowie tried to persuade his backing group, the Spiders From Mars, drawn from the blues-rock circuit in Hull, that the future lay in lipstick, satin and tat, he was met with an initial point-blank refusal. 'It was a big jump from being a blues band in T-shirts and jeans with long hair and beards to wearing make-up and flashy clothes,' insists bassist Trevor Bolder. 'That's one hell of a jump that is. Mick Ronson said, "Bugger that, I'm not dressing up like that."' So Bowie took them along to London's Rainbow Theatre in November 1971, where Alice Cooper was making his British debut, in an attempt to change their minds.

Critically the performance was not a success. 'Alice Cooper is the crescendo and finale in gift-wrapped emptiness,' decided the *Melody Maker*, while *The Times* drew unfavourable comparisons with the support act: 'there was a lack of the sort of theatrical excitement which Arthur Brown had provided.' And Bowie himself very rapidly distanced himself from what he claimed was the artifice of Alice: 'I find him very demeaning,' he proclaimed in 1972; 'it's very premeditated.' But at the time, Bowie's excursion paid instant dividends. 'They were wearing make-up on stage and they were really heavy,' remembers Bolder. 'The music they were playing was great and it didn't look too bad, so we agreed to do it.' And, like it or not, Bowie was to be identified with Alice, the *Melody Maker* review of *Hunky Dory* pointing out that 'he belongs to that oeuvre which Alice Cooper occupies'.

Overleaf

Roxy Music - *Roxy Music* (1972)
The poster for the first Roxy Music album combined the full spread of the gatefold sleeve with the images of the band from the inside of the sleeve. Designer Nick De Ville had studied alongside Bryan Ferry at Newcastle.

Photography Karl Stoecker; design Nicholas De Ville (Island Records)
20 x 30 inches, 76 x 50.5cm

FIRST ALBUM BY ROXY MUSIC [ILPS 9200] OUT NOW

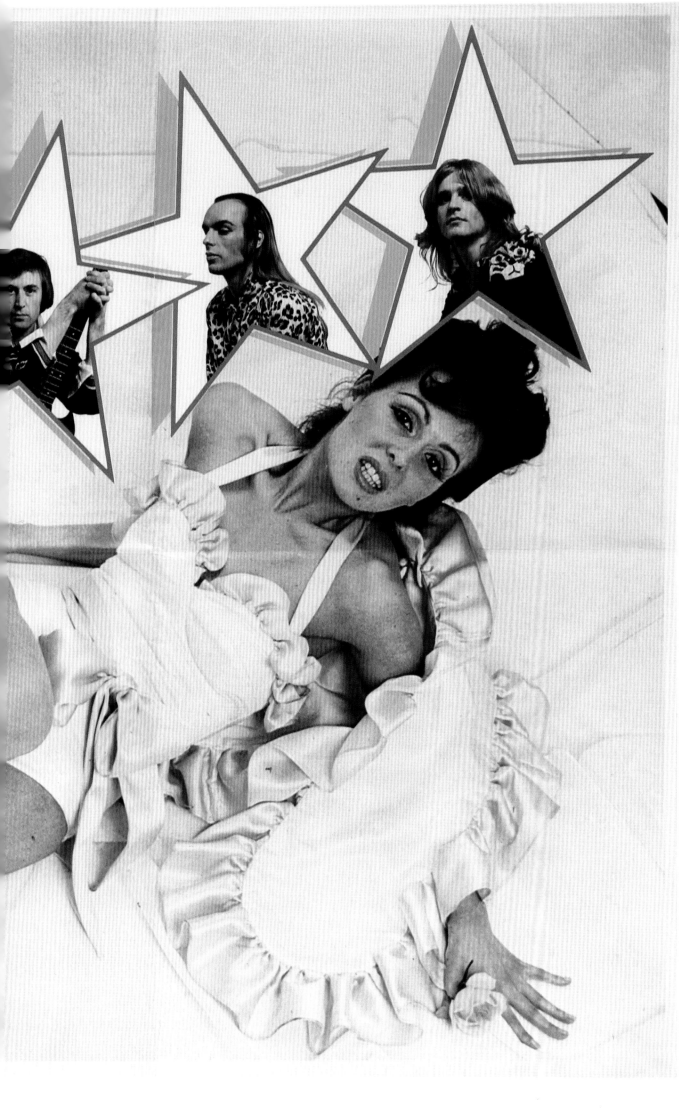

Left

Bryan Ferry (c.1974)

Above

Marc Bolan - *Electric Warrior* insert (1971)
At the high end of glam, the stars existed in a wider context than that of music. Bowie fans would read books and check out movies on his recommendation – he became, in effect, an arbiter of taste. Similarly these portraits of glam stars at home set a tone for fans. 'We'd get this poster and a magnifying glass to find out what cigarettes he was smoking,' says Marco Perroni. 'Even the cigarettes were really good, because they were all white. It was an important statement.'

Left
(Pace International, Holmes McDougall Ltd, Glasgow) 24 x 37 inches, 94.5 x 62cm
Above
(Fly Records) 22 x 30 inches, 76 x 56cm

Bowie's arrival in the British top 10 as a glam star – as opposed to his earlier 1969 incarnation as a vaguely folkie type singing what was assumed to be a novelty hit, 'Space Oddity' – came some eighteen months after Bolan in July 1972. The following month a *Record Mirror* article on a new band had a headline that celebrated what was to become the British glam trinity: 'Bolan, Bowie . . . and now Roxy Music: It's all part of the reaction against Levi's and plimsolls'.

Bolan, Bowie and Roxy Music (particularly Bryan Ferry and Brian Eno) between them established a framework for rock that was startlingly new, whilst being firmly rooted in the past. All in their mid-20s, this was a generation of musicians who had lived through mod and psychedelia, and were now achieving their first commercial success at a time when the sounds of their primary-school years were enjoying a revival. More than any who had gone before, they were aware of their place in a new-found tradition, aware that there was a history of rock & roll, and aware too that this was a music that was never meant to have any such history. Even Elvis himself, way back in 1956, had talked of rock as a passing fad, comparable to the Charleston craze of the '20s. Yet here it was, at sweet little sixteen years of age, and the potency of its cheap music was still extraordinary. The response of the glam generation was to celebrate superficiality. 'We're twentieth-century electric cosmic rock stars!' exclaimed Bolan in 1971, in a teen-pop take on a Futurist manifesto. 'We should be projected and we should be exciting, because it's a fast world. Whether they're deep or shallow, you take your pleasures fast these days.'

THE FANTASTIC SLADE

124 The Slade © Splash Posters Ltd., Splash House Landseer Road, London N19. (01-272 4433)

Ferry, meanwhile, who'd been taught by the British pop artist Richard Hamilton at Newcastle University, introduced the veneer of advertising to the art of album covers: 'I knew that pictures of pretty girls had been used to sell cars, soap and just about everything else. So why not rock music?' he said, adding: 'Advertising images were what had intrigued me as much as anything.' The first Roxy Music sleeve in 1972 featured a cheesy pin-up photograph of model Kari-Ann taken by ex-pat American Karl Stoecker, whose background, revealingly, lay not in music but in the high-gloss world of fashion photography. Inside the gatefold were individual shots of the band members (superimposed on the poster for the album), wearing black Lurex in a variety of synthetic prints. The combined effect was of a retro-future, a '50s vision of a sci-fi world. The group looked as though they had emerged from the cylindrical changing capsules in Mary Quant's 1960s boutique, stepping out into an alternate universe.

Above

The Fantastic Slade (c.1973)

Above - Right

Lost Worlds Festival (1971)

In November 1971 Slade scored their first #1 hit in Britain with 'Coz I Luv You'. The rapidity of their success, after years of toiling on the club circuit, meant that there were still a number of previously booked engagements that weren't necessarily appropriate for a band of their new-found stature Amongst them was the Lost Worlds Festival in December, where they topped a bill comprising Squid, Pigsty Hill Light Orchestra and Birth. The two-colour screen printed poster was characteristic of the period, as was, in a completely different way, the high-street poster produced at the height of Slade's glam success: the dislocation between the rock world of festivals and the *Top of the Pops* studio is here graphically emphasized.

Above
(Higginson & Harris Ltd, London) 20 x 30 inches, 115 x 76cm
Above - Right
23.25 x 31 inches, 79 x 59cm

A similar theme was explored on Bowie's album of the same year, *Ziggy Stardust*, on the sleeve of which he was seen posing in a backstreet in the West End of London wearing a sci-fi costume. In case the point wasn't sufficiently clear, the back of the sleeve showed him in a phone box – Clark Kent's preferred venue for transformation – wearing the same outfit. Again, like the sleeve of *Hunky Dory*, these black and white pictures were colourized by Main Artery (Terry Pastor was the man wielding the airbrush), giving a comic-book feeling to the image.

Bowie also brought to the glam party a gay liberationist perspective, gleaned from his experience in London nightlife with his then wife and mentor, Angie. The most obvious manifestation was on the original British sleeve to his 1971 album *The Man Who Sold The World*, where he appeared in a dress made by designer Mr Fish, but the ambisexual ambivalence of Ziggy also drew on the same well-spring; it was slightly more than coincidence that Bowie's first glam hit, 'Starman', appeared in the top 10 just as the first Gay Pride march was staged in London.

This demonstration, it's worth noting, was organized by the Gay Liberation Front, whereas later Pride marches were the responsibility of the Campaign for Homosexual Equality. There is a key shift in attitude revealed by the names of the respective organizations: the CHE was seeking equal status before the law, where the GLF had grown out of the '60s counter-culture and espoused a much more radical, and simultaneously more pluralist, philosophy of personal and social revolution. Bowie never fitted into an orthodox gay agenda of politics, but his persona, his very existence, in 1971–73 made perfect sense in the context of the contemporary slogan: 'There are as many sexes as there are people.' When he announced to the *Melody Maker* in January 1972 that 'I'm gay, and always have been,' he became the first mainstream rock artist to identify himself with the nascent movement, and the famous Mick Rock photograph of him on stage simulating fellatio on his beautiful guitarist Mick Ronson changed perceptions of what a rock star could be and do.

Even more importantly, his *Top of the Pops* appearance with arm lovingly draped round Ronson was one of the key events in British gay history. Male bonding on this level, in front of eight million viewers, was a drastic departure for television.

It was also an indication of how powerful the medium of TV was in the story of glam. Unlike previous – and subsequent – developments in rock & roll, glam didn't have an incubation period in clubs, patiently building a following and paying its dues. There had been some early ventures, but they made little impression: in early 1970, for example, Bowie had played a gig at the Roundhouse in London under the group name Hype, with the band members dressed in superhero costumes, and the same year had released the proto-glam single 'The Prettiest Star', with Bolan on guitar. But these were isolated and unsuccessful incidents. When Roxy Music played their debut gig at a friend's Christmas party in 1971, they were heckled by an audience member demanding that they play some rock & roll, to which Bryan Ferry coolly replied: 'We *are* rock & roll.'

Apart from these moments, glam was effectively incubated under the studio lights at *Top of the Pops*. Bolan, Slade and Gary Glitter each turned the show into a home-from-home in the early '70s, and the Bowie-Ronson double-act was matched in terms of impact by the debut of Sparks in the spring of 1974, when Ron Mael's piercing stare sent viewers fleeing in terror behind their sofas. This time round, the revolution was televised. Glam simply didn't exist until it reached the small screen in the living room.

Inevitably, therefore, the development of television helped shape the image and presentation of the music. 'Few Englishmen would care to be reminded,' wrote Auberon Waugh in his novel *A Bed of Flowers*, 'that as recently as the night of 31 March 1966, there was no colour television in the British Isles.' Even when it did arrive, colour TV took a long time spreading; by 1972 only 12 per cent of British homes had colour, and the shrewder musicians were well aware of the fact. 'The silver coat used to work great on a black-and-white TV 'cos people didn't need colour to see it, it would reflect,' remembers Dave Hill, the image-conscious guitarist of Slade. 'I thought colour might screw it up for me, 'cos when the colour telly came in I wondered about the colours that we were wearing, but silver's like a universal colour. It's a bit like black or white. There are some colours that do not work, but silver – like white – will hit you.'

In addition to these influences on glam – the lipstick, the rock & roll revival, the Hollywood fantasies, the celebration of the history of popular culture in a defiantly showbiz manner, gay liberation, the use of television – there was one other vital element that combined much of the above: a very specific image of what rock stardom itself entailed.

It starts with '50s rocker Vince Taylor. Despite recording one of the few British rock & roll classics in 'Brand New Cadillac', Taylor had failed to translate a cult live following into chart success, and at the start of the '60s he moved to Paris, where he became a national star. Dressed in black leather, with a chain wrapped around his fist, his was an iconic presence, and for a while he was the biggest draw in French rock. And then he turned on, tuned in, dropped out, and became one of the first acid casualties. By the time Bowie met him in 1966, Taylor (born Brian Holden) had taken to calling himself Mateus, had ambitions to build a new Atlantis and variously claimed to be the son of God and/or an alien. 'He was the inspiration for Ziggy,' Bowie was to acknowledge, later adding: 'I'm not sure if I held him up as an idol or as something not to become. Bit of both probably.'

Another who met Taylor was the future Gary Glitter, who shared a bill with him on a 1960 tour and learnt at his leather-clad knee the golden rule of stardom: 'To him, a rock & roller's image was everything, and he believed you shouldn't let the public see you as your real self, because you'd never appear special to them again.' (The same lesson was later passed on to Adam Ant by Taylor's drummer, Don Hawkins.)

Amongst the many tales told of Taylor, both in wonder and sorrow, Dave Dee remembered him in his French heyday starting his act chained inside a cage while being whipped by two stagehands. It was a staging that recurred in the 1967 Peter Watkins film, *Privilege*, in which Paul Jones played Steven Shorter, a pop star exploited by the British State to keep the masses quiescent, and ultimately turned into a saviour machine. Though the movie was intended primarily as political comment, the most striking feature actually turned out to be Shorter himself; a riddle wrapped in a mystery inside an enigma, with no apparent interest in anything, including his own music, he was the first rock star to be depicted as morally, emotionally and physically helpless, acted upon but unable to initiate action. Jean

Shrimpton co-starred as Vanessa, an artist hired to paint his portrait, but failing to find any internal reality to capture.

'The flashbulbs hurt my eyes now,' Shorter confesses to Vanessa, as he starts to crack up under the strain of being all things to all kids. 'When I started I couldn't get enough of it. When I try to fall asleep now, my eyes hurt. The bulbs keep popping – like bits of glass . . . And they keep reaching out for me. All those hands.' Five years later, Bowie's Vince Taylor-inspired account of the end of stardom, 'Rock & Roll Suicide', provided an uncanny echo of the image: 'You're wonderful – gimme your hands!'

The vision of the reclusive rock star, jaded into near-narcolepsy, not so much killing time as watching it die, was revived and amplified in Mick Jagger's portrayal of Turner in *Performance* (1970), and in the closing scenes of *Stardust* (1974), where David Essex reprised his role as Jim Maclaine from *That'll Be The Day*. Now a superstar recluse, Maclaine – a thousand years on from his days as a ted – dresses entirely in white and lives with his road manager, Mike (played by Adam Faith), in a Spanish castle, spending his time, in the words of the novel: 'sitting on the balcony in a rocking chair snorting coke or wandering around the battlements like some lunatic Hamlet'.

It was a key image in creating the self-conscious decadence at the heart of glam (Gary Glitter, incidentally, had put himself up for the role of Shorter in *Privilege*), and it reached its apotheosis in Alan Yentob's 1975 BBC documentary *Cracked Actor*, with a coked-out Bowie demonstrating no contact whatsoever with reality. It was his performance as himself in that programme that spurred Nicolas Roeg, co-director of *Performance*, to cast Bowie as a masochistic, messianic alien in *The Man Who Fell To Earth* (1976).

This was one strand of glam stardom, but there was another, also identified in Ray Connolly's *Stardust*. In 1964, as Cassius Clay takes on the seemingly hopeless task of removing the world heavyweight boxing title from Sonny Liston, Mike knows which side he's on: 'He would just love it if Clay could win. The world needed a giant-killer. He needed an idol.' Years later, in a wholly different world, Alice Cooper espoused the same emotion: 'Look at Cassius Clay,' he demanded in 1971. 'He must have worn make-up. I wanted him to nail Frazier. He's so obnoxious I really like him.'

Vice. And Versa.

Mick Jagger. And Mick Jagger.

James Fox. And James Fox.

See them all in a film about fantasy. And reality. Vice. And versa.

Hear **Mick Jagger** sing his own song "Memo From Turner."

performance.

James Fox / Mick Jagger / Anita Pallenberg / Michele Breton
Written by Donald Cammell / Directed by Donald Cammell & Nicolas Roeg / Produced by Sanford Lieberson in Technicolor.
A Goodtimes Enterprises Production from Warner Bros. THIS FILM IS RATED X NO ONE UNDER 17 ADMITTED
Hear Mick Jagger sing "Memo From Turner" in the original sound track album on Warner Bros. Records and tapes.

The naming was wrong – Cassius Marcellus Clay, all-American gold medallist of the 1960 Olympics, had reinvented himself as the Black Muslim anti-hero Muhammad Ali – but the identification of him as a glam precursor was absolutely right. His professional ability (he was the greatest in the world), his image (he was beautiful), and above all his attitude (he told everyone that he was the greatest and that he was beautiful) were the very essence of glam. If he didn't wear lipstick, it was only because he was so pretty that he didn't have to.

Left

Performance (1970)
So controversial was the violence, sexual ambiguity and moral relativism of *Performance* ('Nothing is true, everything is permitted') that its release was delayed for two years. This poster dates from its US release (the UK release came in 1971) and was 'Licensed for display only in connexion with the exhibition of this picture . . .'
  Nicolas Roeg later directed *The Man Who Fell To Earth*, images from which were used on the sleeves of Bowie's albums *Station To Station* and *Low* (see pp.60 & 56).

(Warner Brothers Inc) 27 x 41 inches, 79 x 59cm

Right

Rolling Stones - 1973 European Tour (1973)
John Pasche was nearing the end of his course at the Royal College of Art in 1970, when Mick Jagger came to the College asking if there were any particularly talented students who would be interested in designing some artwork for the Stones. Pasche's work impressed Jagger, and his first commission was for the 1970 European tour poster, followed by one for the 1972 American tour. His most famous piece for the band, however, was the tongue-and-lips logo for the band's record label.
  This piece is a pop art reinterpretation of René Magritte's 'Le Viol' ('The Rape', 1934), the original of which was later to appear on an early Adam & the Ants flyer (p.115)

Design John Pasche; photography David Thorpe
(Rolling Stones) 23 x 33 inches, 84 x 59cm

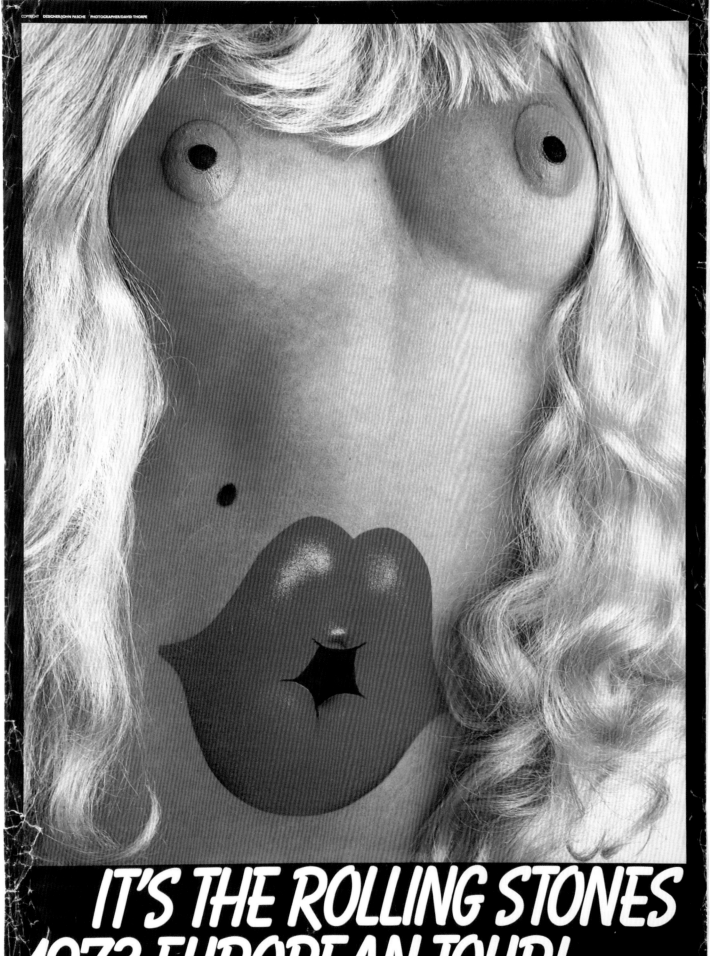

IT'S THE ROLLING STONES 1973 EUROPEAN TOUR!

David Bowie

2
THE GOLDEN AGE OF ROCK & ROLL

We've been around a long time just tryin' to make the big time.
Roxy Music, *'Virginia Plain'* (Bryan Ferry, 1972)

The psychedelic poster moved predictably out of the Underground and spread across the walls of almost every middle-class teenage bedroom.
George Melly, *Revolt Into Style* (Allen Lane, London, 1970)

Ugly, everyone he saw was ugly. Except the doll people of course. Slim and perfect, dressed in weird but becoming fashions, they floated past him. Their transistors, hanging by straps from their necks or wrists, blared out pop music, and their long-lashed doe eyes blinked dopily.
Richard Carlile, *Drummer* (Tandem, London, 1971)

If Marc Bolan had played John the Baptist, it was the appearance of David Bowie as the Leper Messiah on *Top of the Pops* that marked the real start of glam. 'Starman' entered the British top 50 in June '72, at the same time as a trio of other key singles: Slade's 'Take Me Bak 'Ome', their first self-written, full-on stomping hit; Sweet's 'Little Willy', on which they began to transcend the pure bubblegum tendencies of their first successes; and Gary Glitter's 'Rock & Roll (Part 2)'. Within weeks, these records were joined by top 5 hits from Mott The Hoople, Alice Cooper and Roxy Music, and for the first time, there was a sense of a new era in pop, as Noddy Holder recognized: 'The press invented the term glam rock when Sweet changed their sound and Gary Glitter came along.'

For the next two years, glam dominated the charts, with the British public displaying a seemingly insatiable appetite for a music that covered all the bases, from pure, disposable pop through to literate avant-garde rock & roll. At one end of the spectrum was the songwriting – and sometimes production – team of Mike Chapman and Nicky Chinn, whose success was quite extraordinary. Their first hit, the eminently forgettable 'Funny Funny' by Sweet, gave little indication that just three years later, in February 1974, they would be occupying the top three positions on the *NME* charts, with singles by Mud, Suzi Quatro and Sweet; that year they managed to sell more records than the Beatles had managed in any one year.

At the other extreme was Lou Reed, co-opted into glam by Bowie, producer of the 1972 album *Transformer* with its accompanying hit, 'Walk On The Wild Side'. The songs on that album mostly referred back to the New York of the '60s, when Reed had led the Velvet Underground under the patronage of Andy Warhol, providing an artistic and historical lineage for glam, as well as injecting a note of authenticity: if British glam gave the impression of playing a role, Reed's appeal was a sense of unflinching honesty, an impression that he lived this life of alternative sexuality and drug abuse for real.

In between came a host of others: the twisting tales told by Steve Harley and Cockney Rebel, the mock-menace of Alvin Stardust, the Spector-esque pantomime of Roy Wood and Wizzard, the ventripotent vamping of Gary Glitter, the camp theatricalism of Jobriath, the vaudeville intensity of the Sensational Alex Harvey Band. Just as every American TV detective of the '70s had to have a gimmick (the bald one, the scruffy one, the one in the wheelchair), so every glam act had its own take on the dressing-up culture.

It wasn't exactly a new generation. The part played in the creation of glam by the rock & roll revival gave new hope to many of a certain vintage, including Roy Wood, Alvin and Gary. The last two had started their recording careers before the

SUPPORT BAND + BE-BOP DELUXE

LOCARNO NEW BRISTOL CENTRE. BRISTOL

TUES. 26 JULY DOORS OPEN 7·30ᵖᵐ

ADV. TKTS 85ₚ INC VAT. EXPANSION RECORDS 54 PARK ST. BRISTOL

£1· ON DOOR INC. VAT.

Cockney Rebel – Live (1975)

Adapted from the cover photo on the second Cockney Rebel album, *The Psychomodo*, this version trims out the rest of the band to leave only the image of Steve Harley. In fact the rest of the personnel had already left and the act was by now being billed as Steve Harley & Cockney Rebel, under which name they had had a #1 single with 'Make Me Smile (Come Up and See Me)' earlier in the year. The logo for the band's name was also out of date, having existed only on the first two albums.

The original shot was the work of Mick Rock, one of the most celebrated chroniclers of the era, and the man responsible for the definitive images of Iggy, Lou Reed and Bowie (and director of promo films of the latter, including 'The Jean Genie').

Photography Mick Rock; design unknown (Locarno, Bristol) 20 x 30 inches, 76 x 50.5cm

Overleaf - Left

Mick Ronson – *Slaughter on 10th Avenue* (1974)

When the Spiders From Mars split, MainMan pushed guitarist Mick Ronson as a solo star. This poster showed an expanded version of the photo originally used on the album, replaced the typefaces with a less interesting font and added a wholly superfluous drawing of a New York street sign.

Photography & original album design Leee Black Childers (RCA Records & Tapes) 18.5 x 27 inches, 69 x 47cm

Overleaf - Right

Eno – *Here Come The Warm Jets* (1974)

'To be honest, I don't like advertising campaigns,' said Brian Eno in 1978. 'They make me nervous, because I think all that can happen when you do that is disappoint people.'

The sleeve to his first solo album showed a jumble of objects arranged on a shelving unit, with only a small photograph of the artist. The poster for the album and its accompanying tour ignored that artwork entirely to present a darker, more exotic image that pushed Eno's glam image. Even the lettering from the album sleeve was jettisoned in favour of a sleek typeface that drew on the contemporary art deco revival. One of the women pictured is Judy Nylon, later of the art-punk band Snatch.

(Island Records) 20 x 29 inches, 73 x 50.5cm

Beatles; indeed Glitter was older than three of the Beatles, though that paled in comparison with Alex Harvey, who was even older than Tommy Steele himself, the first ever British rocker. All enthusiastically embraced the new era summed up by Gary: 'The whole purpose of glam was to reintroduce a sense of theatre to rock and to have some fun by exaggerating certain elements of pop music presentation.'

Cynical critics suggested that the endorsement of cosmetics might stem from a desire to conceal the signs of ageing, but what glam certainly offered was a sense that stardom was back in fashion and that it was available to the most unlikely of candidates. Such was the overheated atmosphere of the time that even when Mick Ronson emerged from under Bowie's eye-shadow, and when Eno flounced out of Roxy Music, both were heavily marketed in 1974 as ready-made stars-in-waiting: Ronson's debut solo gig was at the prestigious Rainbow Theatre, where membership of his fan club was already on offer. Neither of these campaigns was noticeably successful (Eno, paradoxically, only saw his profile rise in any sustainable way when he began, John Cage-like, to withdraw his personality from his music), but the promotion of side-men in such a way was indicative of how broad the church of glam was. More characteristic of mainstream rock was the tone of apologetic muso-dom captured in the title of Ron Wood's 1974 solo LP, *I've Got My Own Album To Do*. Glam was never so self-effacing.

Despite this widespread adoption of slap and tinsel, the glam generations didn't have it all their way. Primarily there was the problem of America, a market that was reluctant to accept men in make-up: there were places where the new sounds were embraced, but they tended to be clustered on the coasts, particularly in New York and in Los Angeles. The latter saw the inauguration in 1972 of Rodney's English Disco, set up by Anglophile Rodney Bingenheimer who bought posters back from trips to London to staple to the walls. 'There was a series of booths in the club,' he says, 'and each one featured posters of different British pop stars: Mick Jagger, Sweet, T. Rex, Bowie, and Roxy Music. We also had posters in the bathroom. I had a great poster of Suzi Quatro in the women's toilet but it got stolen; Joan Jet spoke to me a few years ago and said that she stole it.' Rodney's became a holiday home for visiting bands and journalists but, despite Bingenheimer's endless enthusiasm, failed to break glam in the States.

Even Bowie himself had trouble converting concert success into record sales in the heartlands of the US, where his sexuality was suspect. And the position wasn't helped by a confusion amongst the artists themselves over who or what exactly constituted glam: 'I did three or four shows like that,' insisted Reed, 'then it was back to leather. We were just kidding around – I'm not into make-up.' And even at the singles end of the market it found no favour: 'We were always a rock band at heart,' remembered Brian Connolly of Sweet; 'glam was just a tag that came along and we rode it shamelessly.' Similarly Dave Hill of Slade denies the description – 'I don't think we were a glam band' – while Suzi Quatro is even more definite: 'I was the anti-glam!'

**HIS NEW ALBUM –
'HERE COME THE WARM JETS'**
Record ILPS 9268 · Cassette ZCI 9268 · Cartridge Y8I 9268

island records

Nonetheless, there was a common approach shared by all: from the high concept artists like Bowie and Ferry through to the most critically reviled pop acts, there was an overwhelming emphasis on visual presentation not necessarily at the expense of, but ideally in complement to, the music. And the more astute realized at an early stage the power of the poster. The first biography of Bryan Ferry (written by Roxy Music's publicist Simon Puxley, under the name Rex Balfour) told the story of how the band commissioned artist Malcolm Bird even before they played a public gig:

The only piece of Roxy artwork done before the inception of their official career in February 1972 had been a wall poster showing in multiple an airplane above skyscrapers tracing out the legend 'Roxy Music': no place, no date (because there weren't any), no hint of what it all meant, just the name enigmatically presented sixty times over. Bryan and the others had posted them around London ...

Above

Lou Reed - Spring Tour (1975)
After the success of *Rock & Roll Animal*, a further set of live tracks was issued as *Lou Reed Live*. The album wasn't as strong but the cover image – which dated from the 1974 tour – was a classic, with Reed seen in a studded outfit that emphasized New York's continuing love affair with the black leather jacket. ('But that fucking hat! Ugh!' says John Holmstrom, who based his illustration for the cover of *Punk* #1 on this image - see p.76.)

Photography Oliviero Toscani; design Acy R Lehman; concept Dennis Katz (RCA Records & Tapes) 20 x 36 inches, 91.5 x 51cm

Right

Lou Reed – Berlin (1973)
The poster for *Berlin* returns to the original concept of the record. Intended to be a double album, with gatefold sleeve and a booklet that would illustrate the story of the songs, the project was downscaled by RCA to a single album with a lyric sheet insert. The photographs that were taken for the booklet were recycled for use on the movie-theme poster to make the point that this was 'A film for the ear'.

The concept enabled some heavyweight name-dropping – Jack Bruce, Steve Winwood et al – designed to help Reed's claim to being a major artist (earlier promotional material had made much of Bowie's endorsement for the same reason). The advance quote of *Rolling Stone*'s Larry Sloman wasn't matched by the negative review the album got in the magazine on release.

Photography Saint Jivago Desanges (RCA Records & Tapes) 24 x 37 inches, 94 x 61cm

Overleaf - Left

Lou Reed – *Coney Island Baby* (1976)
The repetition of the album cover on the poster is a conscious reference to Andy Warhol's work, but the original photo also echoes the imagery of *Cabaret*. Others who drew on the influence of Broadway included the Sensational Alex Harvey Band who covered 'Tomorrow Belongs To Me' from the same show, and Alice Cooper, whose *School's Out* album included elements from *West Side Story*.

Bowie's connection with *Cabaret* was more direct, befriending writer Christopher Isherwood (on whose work the show was based), having perhaps recognized a kindred spirit in the man who wrote: 'I am a camera with its shutter open, quite passive, recording, not thinking.'

Photography Mick Rock (RCA Records & Tapes) 24 x 36 inches, 91.5 x 61cm

Overleaf - Right

Lou Reed - *Rock & Roll Animal* (1974)
The sleeve to Reed's live album showed him from chest upwards. In the transferral of this to a poster format it appears that another photo of him from waist downwards has been spliced onto a fuller version of the original shot, giving a distorted and slightly disturbing picture.

Photography Dalrymple; design Acy R Lehman (RCA Records & Tapes) 24 x 36 inches, 91.5 x 61cm

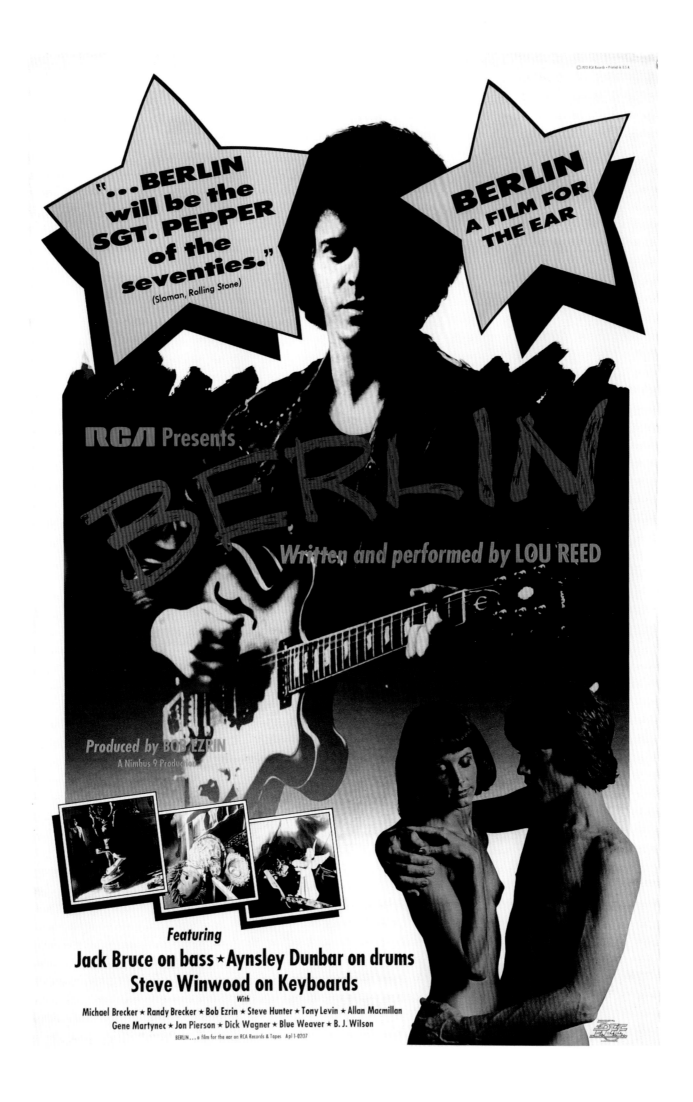

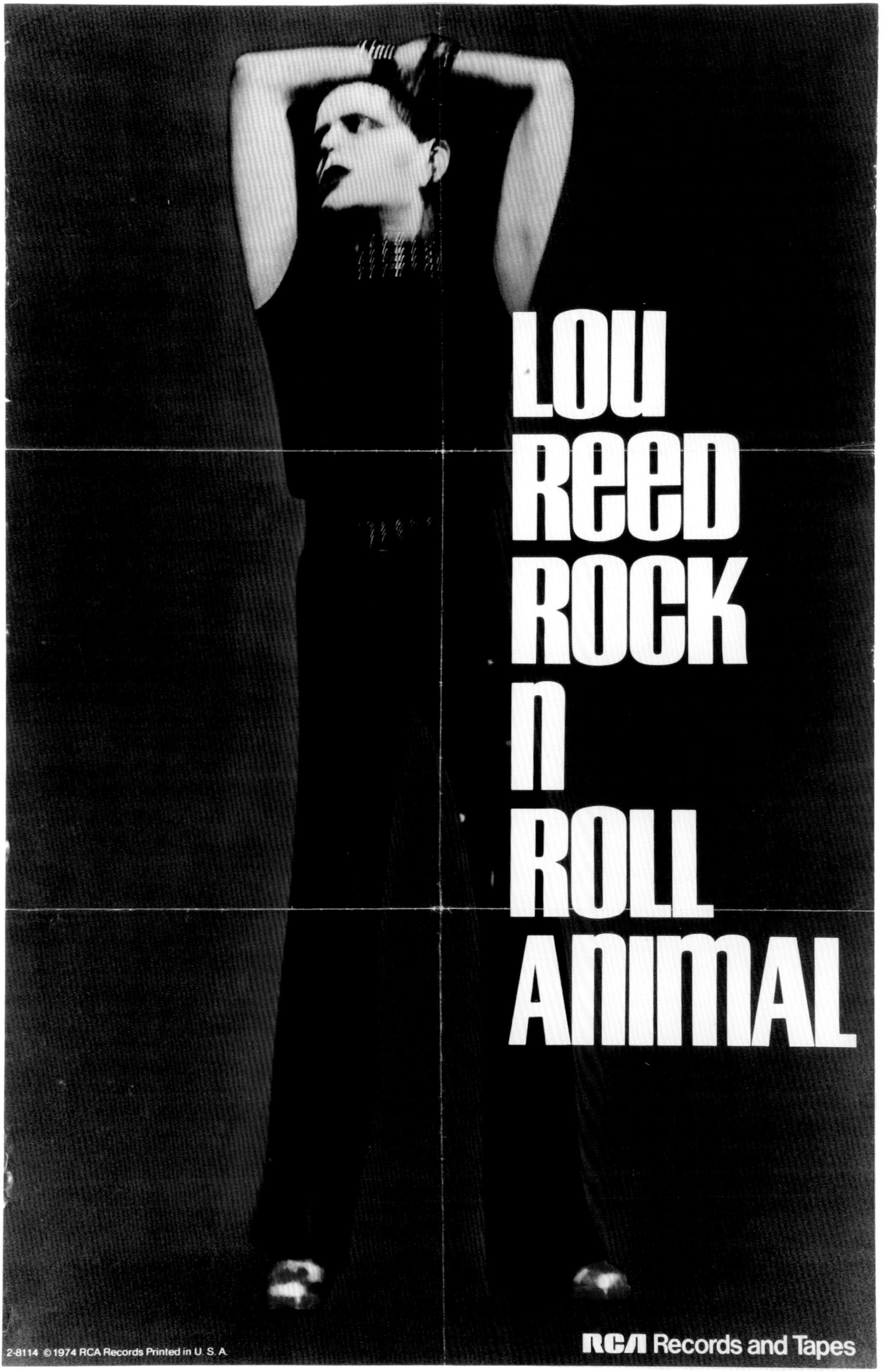
LOU
REED
ROCK
n
ROLL
ANIMAL
RCA Records and Tapes
2-8114 © 1974 RCA Records Printed in U. S. A.

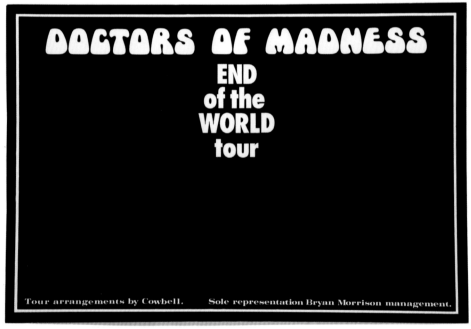

Left

Sparks – Live (1974)
This gig, in the wake of Sparks's first UK hit 'This Town Ain't Big Enough For Both Of Us', was staged in a temporary venue near Plymouth Argyle's stadium at Home Park. The typeface for the word Sparks is Shatter by Letraset. The format – a one-colour screen print on landscape double crown paper (20 x 30 inches) – was standard: this was the mainstay of gig posters for a decade.

(Vandike Organization) 20 x 30 inches, 76 x 51cm

Left

Doctors of Madness – Live (1976)
One of the great neglected bands in British rock, the Doctors of Madness spanned the gulf between glam and punk but never quite made it. For such a visually striking band (singer Kid Strange had blue hair, while bassist Stoner adopted Frankenstein make-up and Urban Blitz played the violin) this is a remarkably anti-image poster. It is also a difficult one on which to fill in gig information, since the blank strip is black.

20 x 30 inches, 76 x 50.5cm

Right

New York Dolls – *New York Dolls* (1973)
The original photo session for the album sleeve was staged in a Third Avenue antique shop and was loathed by the band; 'To me it was a piece of shit,' commented guitarist Sylvain Sylvain. The alternative that the band created took on both glam and the Stones and trumped them both with an instant classic, a shot that oozed sleaze, decadence and glamour and provided a template for rock bands for decades to come. 'The first album was a classic,' Suicide singer Alan Vega once remarked. 'What a cover!'

Photography Toshi (Mercury Records) 32.5 x 44 inches, 112 x 82.5cm

This elevation of the poster to the status of cultural calling card was prescient. For, by coincidence or otherwise (probably otherwise), the rise of photogenic rock stars in the glam era was staged alongside an explosion of poster production.

In the late '60s the poster had been adopted as an artistic off-shoot of psychedelia, initially in San Francisco, where the first psych-poster exhibition was staged as early as July 1967, and then in London. Primarily designed to promote gigs, these acid-driven variations on art nouveau had been identified almost immediately as works of art, and their creators (Rick Griffin, Stanley Mouse, Wes Wilson amongst others) acclaimed as key figures in the underground.

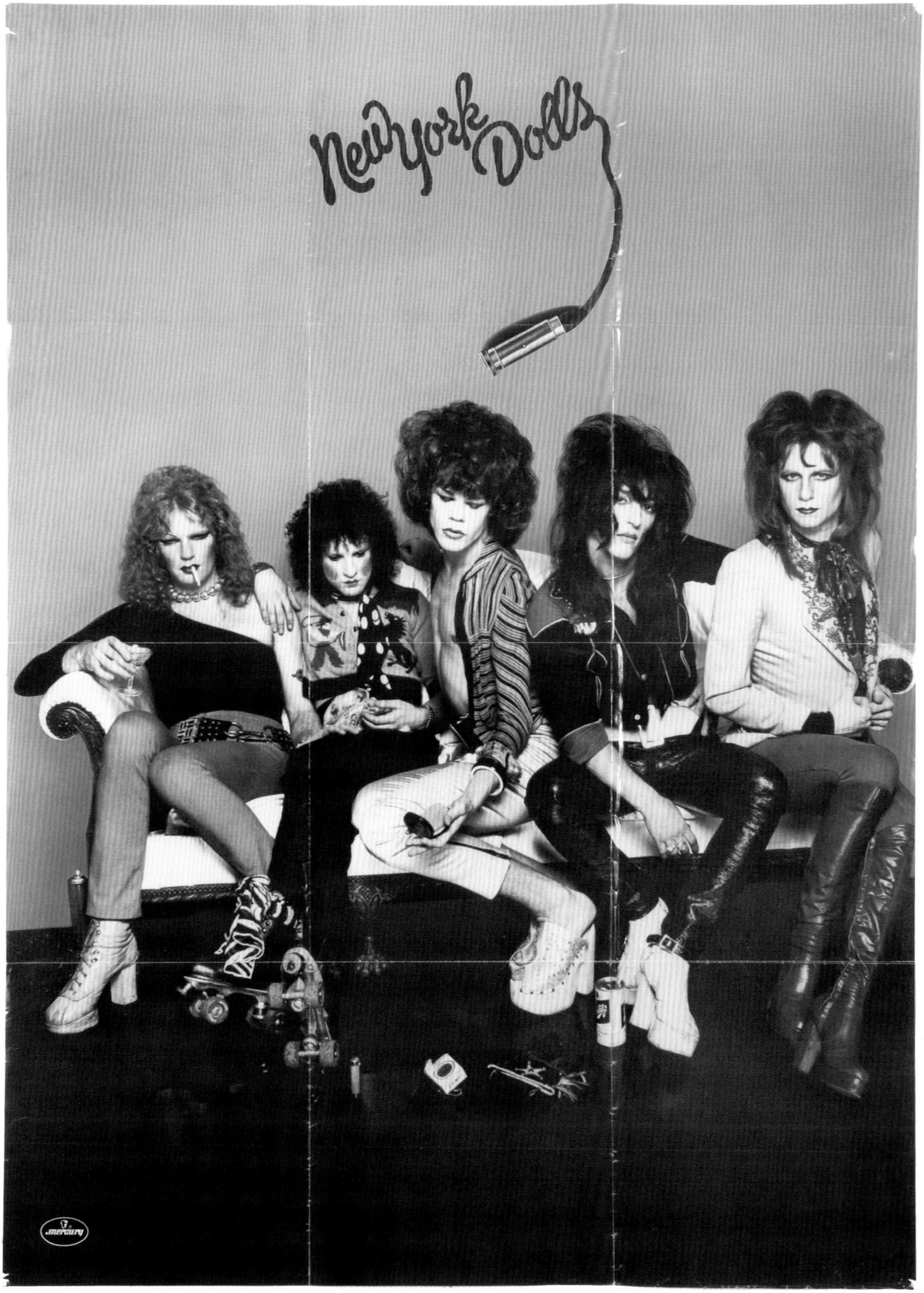
New York Dolls
mercury

SPAR

KIMONO MY HO

RECORD ILPS 9272, CASSETTE ZCI 9272, CARTRIDGE Y8I

Nº1

Left

Sparks – *Kimono My House* (1974)
The cover sleeve of Sparks' third album was a photograph of two members of the Kabuki theatre company that was then visiting London. Since Kabuki tradition doesn't allow for women on stage, the image was a sly use of cross-dressing in the midst of the glam era.

The poster included the sleeve but focussed on an image of the band posing with their name spelt out in light-entertainment style.

Cover concept Ron Mael; art direction Nick De Ville; photography Karl Stoecker (Island Records) 20 x 30 inches, 76 x 51cm

Overleaf – Left

Iggy & the Stooges – *Metallic KO* (1976)
The existence of tapes of the Stooges's last gig had been one of the great legends of rock for some time before the semi-official version emerged on the French label Skydog, hence the 'Mass Suicide Prevented' promotion. The album sleeve was designed by Michael Beal.

(Skydog Records) 22 x 28 inches, 56 x 71cm

MASS SUICIDE PREVENTED!

Often talked about but seldom heard, this amazing Lp captures Iggy & The Stooges at their out-of-control finest. Including such Stooges classics as "Raw Power" and "Gimme Danger", and featuring an impromptu "Louie Louie" (complete with outrageous Pop dialogue), METALLIC KO certifies Iggy & The Stooges' position as the main seminal influence on today's "new wave" bands.

METALLIC KO
IGGY AND THE STOOGES

Available on the
Import Records Label &
GRT music tapes.
IMP 1015

FIRST 15,000 COPIES PRESSED IN BLACK VINYL.

50

In London, similarly, Nigel Waymouth and Michael English – collectively known as Hapshash and the Coloured Coat – were commissioned by the UFO Club to design a series of posters for gigs by the likes of the Move and the Pink Floyd. Joe Boyd, who was running the club, then approached the criminal types who controlled illegal postering in the city and paid them to put up the notices. Within weeks he saw the pieces turning up for sale on the King's Road and realized that you couldn't trust London villains: they'd take your money, put up half the posters and flog the rest to would-be hipsters seeking a piece of the psychedelic action: 'I hated the fact that this godfather was selling posters out of the back of the van,' he remembers. 'And we were paying him to put them up. So he was making money twice…'

More constructively, he also concluded that there was a market for this new artefact. What had been intended as adverts were apparently desirable objects in their own right, statements of belonging; the imagery was becoming a badge of identity, proclaiming the owner as a member of the counter-culture. All of which made Boyd decide that here was a potential business opportunity, and he promptly set up a new company, Osiris, with the intention of making posters and selling them via record shops. It was a sound idea, but Boyd was ahead of his time. The sales infrastructure simply didn't exist, record shops had no facilities for stocking anything other than records, and by the end of 1967, losses had been cut and Osiris had been declared insolvent.

Within this short-lived venture was a significant shift in production. Where the earlier gig posters had been silk-screened – a labour-intensive process suitable only for short runs – these would-be commercial pieces were reproduced using off-set litho, a technique capable of mass-production. Litho was still relatively new to the British industry at the time (the Osiris posters had to be printed in Holland), but over the next couple of years, increasing numbers of printing plants moved from letterpress to off-set, bringing unit costs down and facilitating – as a side-effect – the cheap production of full-colour posters in large print-runs.

The means of distribution, however, still lagged behind. There were a handful of head shops around Britain that were prepared to stock posters, and Big O – one of the earliest poster firms in the country – had a stall in Kensington Market, West London where the future gig-promoter Harvey Goldsmith started his career in the music industry, but high-street shops were thin on the ground. Amongst the exceptions were Athena, which opened its first outlet in Hampstead in 1964, concentrating on the art end of the market, and Biba in Kensington, which not only produced its own posters, but in 1969 also introduced a range of wallpaper sold in poster-sized sheets: it was believed that these would be easier to put up than traditional rolls for Biba's target market, teenage girls setting up home for the first time.

The real breakthrough came in the back pages of the music papers. In 1970 Richard Branson launched Virgin Records as a mail-order discount record retailer, advertising in the *Melody Maker* and introducing the concept of mail-order into rock. His initiative was followed by other record dealers (Comet, Express Record Service, Mail-A-Disc), and by those seeking to off-load crushed velvet loon pants and Afghan coats. By 1972 poster companies like Art Tempo, Art Media and Permaprints had also joined in, and soon thereafter Stick 'Em Up was advertising its own posters (for Bolan, Mott The Hoople, Jimi Hendrix and others) as being available via a network of named shops: these ranged from the counter-cultural Some Kinda Mushroom in Chesterfield to the more orthodox sounding Parson Television Service in Cadoxton. With demand clearly established, the move from the semi-display ads to the high street was inevitable and it wasn't long before the likes of Woolworths were installing poster-display racks into their shops.

The growth of the mass-market litho poster was also assisted by the relative price in the early years. At the start of 1972 a standard-sized 20" x 30" full-colour poster would typically cost around fifty pence, compared to the thirty pence price tag on a single. Two years later, however, inflation had been exacerbated by the rocketing cost of vinyl following on from the oil crisis of late '73, and the differential had reduced considerably; now a single was up to fifty-three pence, with a poster standing at sixty-five pence. For kids who wanted to demonstrate their affinity with a band, the poster on the bedroom wall or in the sixth-form common room was becoming a much more viable option.

Alongside this early flowering of commercially available posters, record companies too were exploiting the off-set litho revolution. Promotional posters had been comparatively rare in the '60s: Hapshash and the Coloured Coat had produced a piece for Tomorrow's debut single 'My White Bicycle', but the initiative for that had come from the band's management rather than from EMI, and the only record company enthusiastically to solicit their services was Track Records, an independent label founded by Kit Lambert and Chris Stamp, which included the Who and Hendrix on its roster. (Indeed it was Track who had encouraged the founding of Osiris, promising that the products would be sold via Track's distribution deal with Polydor; 'When we finally had a meeting with Polydor,' remembers Boyd, 'they said: "You must be joking, we're not going to distribute this stuff, it's not 12 by 12. How would we do that?"')

Promotion was scarce partly because there was little need of it, according to Pete Jenner, the first manager of Pink Floyd and later of Tyrannosaurus Rex:

> I remember that the Floyd were a big hyped band from EMI, and for 'See Emily Play' they took a quarter-page ad, and that was a big deal: to take a quarter-page ad in *Disc* and *Melody Maker*. God knows there were only about a hundred bands in some sense working and doing things, so people knew what was going on. There were probably only about fifty British rock albums released in 1968.

In the more heated market-place of the early '70s, on the other hand, there was an increasing need for bands to shout to make their voices heard, and record shops – which in many British towns were only just emerging from the backrooms of retail outlets primarily selling electrical goods, sweets or musical instruments – began to become inundated with promotional material, intended for short, sharp campaigns. It was also the start of fans walking into their local record shop and asking if they could have the display after it was finished with; no one was quite sure what to do with the things once their working life was over.

The glam generation was the first to benefit from this reinvention of the poster. The development of its artwork can be seen in the complete shift in style on Lou Reed's early solo albums. The first (pre-glam) had had a sleeve painting of a Fabergé egg in an urban street with a confused typeface; his second, the Bowie- and Ronson-produced *Transformer*, had photographs by Mick Rock and Karl Stoecker on the front and back respectively. This focus on the human form and on the artist himself mirrored Bowie's insistence that he should be pictured on every sleeve: every Reed album for the next decade would also have his image on it.

In broad terms, this became the key distinction between glam and its major rival in the early '70s, progressive rock. The Hipgnosis-designed sleeve to Pink Floyd's *Dark Side of the Moon*, for example, and the posters that were enclosed within it, needed to be decoded; they demanded that a viewer recognize the imagery and relate it to a particular record with which – to an outside observer – it had little obvious connection. Similarly, the fantasy landscapes of Roger Dean and Rodney Matthews, artists who produced posters for the company Big O as well as album covers, were considered to be rock solely because of the use to which their work was put.

The bleached-out photo of a haunted, sunken-eyed Reed on the front of *Transformer*, on the other hand, or the submissive, lightning-struck face of Bowie on *Aladdin Sane*, or the dragged-up thrift-shop trash of the New York Dolls – these required little deciphering. They couldn't be mistaken for anything else, couldn't be confused with one of the more elliptical adverts that were then becoming fashionable, but instead were themselves part of rock & roll, speaking directly to the viewer, communicating the style and content of the music inside, in the same way that two decades earlier the very appearance of Little Richard, a black man camping it up in make-up and pompadour hairdo, had proclaimed that he wanted to overturn social norms.

Partly this approach was the consequence of the use of photography at the expense of painting, but mostly it was a change in aesthetics. Glam had little time for the organic writhing of psychedelia nouveau, nor for Tolkien-esque fantasy, nor even for surrealism, all dominant themes of '60s rock artwork. Rather it took its lead from pop art, and particularly from the British version of pop articulated by the likes of Peter Blake, Eduardo Paolozzi and Richard Hamilton.

The emergence of pop art in the 1950s had been a response to American industrial production, exploring mass-culture and drawing on subjects – advertising, Hollywood, commercial architecture and design – beyond the traditional confines of fine art. From a British perspective, this fascination with Americana had from the outset an awareness of absence, experienced as it was at one step's remove through the 2-D representations of movies and magazines, since very few Britons had actually visited the States at this stage. (The situation was still much the same in the pre-Freddie Laker mid-'70s, when Mott The Hoople's Ian Hunter assumed that many of his fans would never even have been

Below
Roxy Music – Poster artwork (1972)
This design by Malcolm Bird was used on the first-ever Roxy Music poster, before the band signed to Island Records, and on stage passes in the early months of the band. At this stage the group was effectively a work in progress and, although this image was superseded by Nick De Ville's later artwork, it did establish a retro look with its bi-plane and deco skyline.

Right
Eno – *Disc* (1974)
This pin-up from the centre-pages of *Disc* magazine (2 February 1974) emphasized the glam credentials of Brian Peter George St John le Baptiste de la Salle Eno, former student at Ipswich Art School and Winchester School of Art.

(*Disc*) 16 x 23.5 inches, 60 x 41.5cm

DISC
PORTRAIT GALLERY SERIES: ENO

SUZI
QUATRO

INTRO
SUZI QUATRO

Suzi Quatro – *Intro* **magazine (c.1974)**
Before punk, Detroit-born Suzi Quatro was pretty much the only role model for young female rock fans. Her competition, such as it was, came from two-way family favourites like Lynsey de Paul and the female half of the New Seekers: flouncy, frilly, feminine. Whereas Suzi describes her image at the time as being 'a very ballsy woman: still feminine but ballsy.'

(*Intro*) 22.5 x 30.75 inches, 78 x 57cm

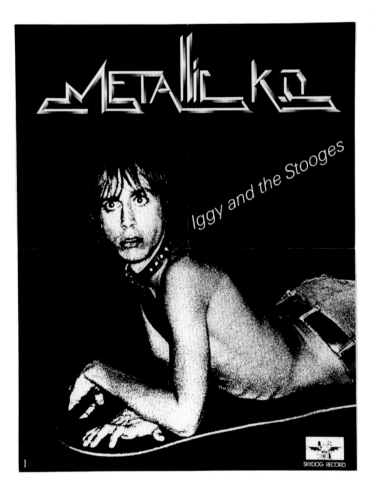

Iggy & the Stooges – *Metallic KO* **(1976)**
A more familiar promotional piece for Iggy than the other poster for *Metallic KO* (p.61).

(Skydog Records) 14 x 18 inches, 45.5 x 35cm

in a plane: 'For those of you who have never flown,' he wrote, 'I can tell you it's a buzz if you can dig it.') In particular, the treatment of movie and music stars was approached ambivalently, with both a spirit of celebration and a sense of distance: these were figures even more remote and untouchable when viewed from the other side of the Atlantic.

The most famous piece of British pop art made this explicit. The sleeve of the Beatles' *Sgt Pepper* album, designed by Peter Blake and Jann Haworth, showed life-sized cut-out depictions of dozens of celebrities in the midst of which, the only living three-dimensional figures, were the Beatles themselves (accompanied by their Madame Tussaud's wax models). The band are consciously placed within a modern pantheon, but there's an acknowledgement too of the absurdity of such an endeavour – these aren't real people surrounding them, but the characters in a shared fantasy.

It was a theme that Bowie was to explore in his glam phase, dropping names that resonated because of the cultural clutter they had acquired, but that also brought an atmosphere of unreality. *Hunky Dory*, for example, has lyrical or musical references to Winston Churchill, Aleister Crowley, Bob Dylan, Kim Fowley, Greta Garbo, Heinrich Himmler, John Lennon, the Mamas and Papas, Mickey Mouse, Lou Reed and Andy Warhol. There is a feeling here of a verbal collage, a technique that is ultimately derived from pop art.

In the context of the rock & roll revival, Marc Bolan's use of a Chuck Berry line at the end of 'Get It On' ('meanwhile, I was still thinking') falls in the same category, as do David Essex's invocation of James Dean in 'Rock On' and Gary Glitter's revivalist shopping list in 'Rock & Roll (Part 1)', name-checking earlier songs including 'Blue Suede Shoes', 'Little Queenie' and 'US Male'. Indeed the ubiquity of the phrase 'rock & roll' itself dates from this period, turning up everywhere from Wizzard ('Rock & Roll Winter') to Bowie ('Rock & Roll With Me') to the Rolling Stones ('It's Only Rock & Roll'). Unlike the lyrics of Don McLean's contemporary 'American Pie', these quotations aren't sewn together in a coherent narrative, but remain isolated incidents, referenced primarily for the external associations they carry. Again, they have no need for intellectual decoding; rather they are triggers, short cuts to a shared culture.

Even more powerful, though, was glam's adoption of pop art's star system. Pop had played on the iconography of Marilyn Monroe, Elvis Presley and Popeye; glam made the logical extension of creating its own icons and then treating them in the same manner. The musicians themselves, complete with make-up and made-up names, became works of art, and none more so than Bowie, whose restless remaking and remodelling presented him as a canvas that was repainted on every sleeve and every poster, a pop palimpsest to be admired, adored and imitated. Making the point clearly was the sleeve of his 1980 album *Scary Monsters and Super Creeps*, where artist Edward Bell – who cites Hamilton and Warhol as influences on the piece – included representations of the cover art from the previous three albums.

And the fact that it was self-conscious was recognized early on. 'Until now, Bowie's never been a star,' commented *Gay News* in 1972, 'but he's studied some of the best, like Garbo and Presley, and now he's on top and he knows what to do.'

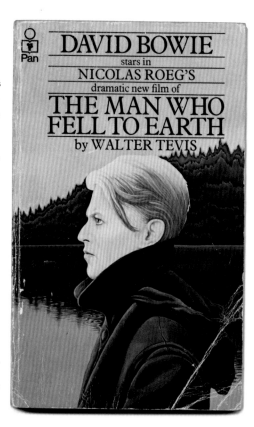

Left
David Bowie – *Low* (1977)
Right
Walter Trevis – *The Man Who Fell To Earth* (1976)
When the novel of *The Man Who Fell To Earth* was reissued to tie in with the movie's release, George Underwood was commissioned to paint the cover. The still that he chose as source material thus became the best-known image of the movie and was subsequently employed on the sleeve of *Low*, offering a familiar hook to sweeten the blow of Bowie's most experimental ever work. The promotional budget for the record was much lower than for previous albums, and the large-format (48 x 48 inches) posters for record stores are amongst the rarest promotional pieces for Bowie in the '70s.

Underwood was a school friend of Bowie (it was his punch that damaged Bowie's left eye) and played guitar in his first recorded band, the King Bees. He subsequently abandoned music in pursuit of a career in art, designing many album sleeves, posters and book jackets.

Left
(RCA Records & Tapes) 20 x 30 inches, 76 x 50.5cm
Right
Painting by George Underwood (Pan paperback)

Right
Bowie – Career overview (1978)
Having taken experimentalism to new heights on *Low* and *Heroes*, Bowie's next album was for RCA's classical label, Red Seal, narrating Prokofiev's *Peter and the Wolf*. Clearly unsure how to promote such an odd departure, RCA responded by issuing a poster that wrapped up his entire work to date for the label.

(RCA Records & Tapes) 20 x 30 inches, 76 x 51cm

The association with pop art wasn't accidental. The aesthetic impulse of glam had largely come from mod, the early 1960s London-based youth cult that numbered both Bolan and Bowie amongst its adherents. 'Despite the fact that they lacked a political programme,' noted Alan Fletcher in his novelization of the Who's movie *Quadrophenia*, 'the mods revolutionized a generation by making it conscious of itself.' And the Who themselves, the archetypal self-conscious mod band, had taken to pop with enthusiasm, employing imagery such as the Union flag and the target, derived from Jasper Johns via Blake, and adopting the trappings of advertising on *The Who Sell Out*.

The key to mod had been the alliance it built between industrial working-class youth and the world of the art student. The Who embodied this tense class coalition even within its line-up: on the one hand there was singer Roger Daltry, an ex-sheet metal worker quite happy to continue a discussion outside; on the other there was guitarist Pete Townshend, fresh out of art school and full of ideas about style. It was characteristic of Townshend, for example, that he first came across mod not on the street but in the *Sunday Times* ('I had to learn how to be a mod,' he later admitted), and of Daltry that he was unconvinced by the posing: he thought the band looked like 'teds in mods' clothing'.

This combination of the urban working class and the art school tradition shaped the music that made the '60s swing, creating the space that was necessary for the Beatles, the Rolling Stones and the Kinks to transcend their rock & roll roots and to embrace art. But it was a fragile unity from the outset, incorporating two very different visions of evading the reality of working-class life: the public escape of hedonistic excess at the weekend, and the private withdrawal into artistic self-expression. The music that jointly expressed these two tendencies coincided for only a short period before the coalition splintered, a break precipitated by the art wing seeking new pastures. A subsequent alliance was briefly built during psychedelia, before that too split.

By the beginning of the '70s a vast gap had opened up between private and public music. Pink Floyd made records that were designed to be listened to on headphones at home, and that were seldom heard in the office or the factory on daytime radio, or on pub jukeboxes, or performed by covers bands in a local club. Similarly, their artwork was

wilfully indirect, speaking to the cognoscenti, emphasizing the private nature of music's appeal. Meanwhile the working-class constituency of mod had evolved into skinhead and northern soul, two subcultures where the focus was on dancing, rather than on creating new music: not a single significant band came out of either tradition until the Specials and Dexys Midnight Runners right at the end of the decade. (Slade had briefly been persuaded to adopt a skinhead image in 1969, but it was a visual gimmick that made no difference to their music – they were never part of skinhead.) Friday night, it appeared, didn't need art in order to provide a release from the working week.

Glam sought to bridge this gap by bringing art-rock back to the charts, echoing the successes of the previous generation of British rock, though there was one notable exception amongst the bands that were referenced: while the Stones and the Who remained relevant, and even at the end of the decade were still influencing the presentational style of, respectively, the Clash and the Jam, the Beatles had to settle for influencing the Pleasers. For much of British rock in the '70s, the Beatles were the dog that didn't bark in the night; so dominant had they been, and yet how peripheral they now seemed, that it was as though there had been a collective decision to send them from Liverpool to Coventry. 'Beatles Reunion' became an urban myth to be clutched at by desperate editors as an alternative to 'Elvis To Tour UK', but their artistic legacy was seen more as a millstone than a touchstone. The Stones, meanwhile, had one last incarnation – as the Greatest Rock & Roll Band in the World – to perfect and to pass on like a poisoned chalice, and the Who, somewhat surprisingly, became the most influential of the '60s bands.

It was, for once, a reciprocated affair: Bowie included two Who songs on his album *Pinups*, while Townshend invited Sweet to be support act for the group's 1974 gig at Charlton Athletic. (The latter never materialized; Sweet singer Brian Connolly got mugged and had his throat kicked in at precisely the wrong moment, and they were replaced on the bill by Maggie Bell.) And when the Who included in their 1970 album *Live at Leeds* a reprint of their Maximum R&B poster from their Marquee days, it was a reminder that they were also the most visually literate of the established bands. This at a time when the '70s poster explosion was about to start again breaking down the barriers that separated spheres of music: essentially produced as a public

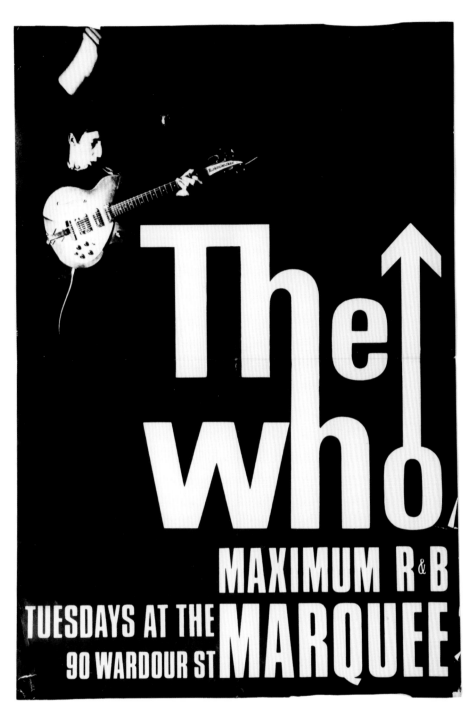

Left

The Who – Maximum R&B (1970)
Originally used to advertise the Who's residency at the Marquee in 1964-65, the reprint of this classic poster came as part of the packaging with their *Live at Leeds* album. Its inclusion there meant that, like the Alice Cooper calendar (p.22), it became a ubiquitous sight on bedroom walls in the new decade: a copy is seen, for example, on the reverse of the Dictators's debut album (p.83)

Design Brian Pike (Track) 20 x 30 inches, 76 x 51cm

advertisement, posters were appropriated by fans as a semi-private, semi-public expression of loyalty and taste.

Like mod, however, glam was not to be a sustainable coalition. In 1972–73 Bowie, Ferry and Reed found themselves alongside Gary Glitter and the Chinnichap acts in the trenches of the glam wars, a situation tolerated only by virtue of the tactical gains it made possible. Glam had become an image that could be attached to, for example, professional wrestling ('Exotic' Adrian Street and 'Bad' Bobby Barnes drew heavily on Mohammad Ali's hero, 1950s US wrestler

DAVID BOWIE'S NEW ALBUM "STATION TO STATION"

STATIONTOSTATIONDAVIDBOWIE

12-9659/B485BN3007 © 1975 RCA Records • Printed in U.S.A.

RC/I Records

Left

David Bowie – *Station To Station* (1976)
One of Bowie's most striking album covers, *Station To Station* featured a still from the movie *The Man Who Fell To Earth*, though the black-and-white rendition and the cropped shape distances it from its source. No longer the alien Thomas Jerome Newton, Bowie looks here like he's stepped from Weimar Germany into a futurist recording studio, suggesting a new, more austere direction to his career. The upper-case sans serif typeface, with no spacing between the words (used again on *ChangesOneBowie*), completes a classic piece of European modernism that would have worked as effectively in the 1930s as it did in the '70s.

The promotional poster compromised this vision by spelling out the title in a more conventional manner, and diluted the impact of the original design. (The movie itself, despite being set in the future, featured posters for Bowie's then current album *Young Americans*.)

Photography Nicolas Roeg (RCA Records & Tapes)
22 x 27.5 inches, 70 x 56cm

Gorgeous George, the 'Human Orchid', to create the glam tag team known as Hell's Angels), and it was evident that vulgarity was outweighing the *fin de siècle* pose of decadence. The more artistically inclined of the glam stars promptly pulled up their skirts and ran, with all the disdain displayed by the style elite through the ages. (On the day that the Prince Regent was crowned as George IV, he had been informed that the mob was not on his side: 'I care nothing for the mob,' he replied, 'but I do for the dandies.')

By the end of 1974 Bowie had jumped ship to catch the coming wave of plastic soul, along with Elton John and Roxy Music; Ferry as a solo artist was retreating into his retro-gigolo persona, while Brian Eno had withdrawn from live performance and virtually from song itself. The winds of change were blowing and Bolan, caught still pouting for the cameras, stayed like that, left behind with the tattered remnants of what had been glam. His 1974 album *Zinc Alloy & The Hidden Riders of Tomorrow* was, he claimed, 'a kind of send-up of Ziggy and Alvin Stardust'. It was two years too late – a lifetime in pop.

Right

Iggy Pop – Commercial poster (1978)
Issued at a time when Iggy was benefiting from the twin patronage of Bowie and the punk establishment, the photo session from which this comes actually dates back to the 1973-74 period when the Stooges were on the West Coast. The long dyed hair, the bow-tie and the hippy jeans (complete with John Pasche's Rolling Stones logo) were in sharp contrast to his then-image, though the physical destruction of rock's legacy chimed with the period's attitudes.

Photography Mirage (One Stop Posters, Los Angeles, licensed through Danny Sugerman) 23 x 35 inches, 88.5 x 58.5cm

EXCLUSIVE DISTRIBUTORS:
...S STOP POSTERS
...9 Exposition Blvd.
...s Angeles, Ca. 90018

IGGY POP

ty vaCant

NEW SINGLE ON VIRGIN RECORDS VS184 1

THE DAMNED

**Album out now.
Play it at your sister.**

32 Alexander Street London W2
"The sound is in the plastic"

RICHARD HELL AND THE VOIDOIDS
THE BLANK GENERATION

TELEVISION

MARQUEE MOON

"HEROES" DAVID BOWIE

METALLIC K.O.
Iggy and the Stooges

A PLATTER OF
RAW IGGY TO GO.

3 SUFFRAGETTE CITIES

Little by little, the city had been drawing all that good juice from him, a little here, a little there, everything going out, nearly every second of the day, the sidewalks at every step drawing something out of him through his feet, the traffic noises sucking at his ears, the neon signs pulling something vital from his eyes...
James Lee Herlihy, *Midnight Cowboy* (Simon & Schuster, New York, 1965)

The room was fairly large, but badly furnished. It boasted only an unmade bed, with a couple of filthy blankets thrown loosely over it, a row of clothes pegs on one wall and two or three planks balanced upon bricks which served as a bookshelf and record rack. A few colourful posters of the Rolling Stones were the only things that lent any brightness to the drab surroundings.
Peter Cave, *Chopper* (NEL, London, 1971)

It was the apartment of a freaked-out musician. There were records and discarded clothes piled everywhere – tables, chairs, even the bed. The walls were covered with posters – record album promotions, dead film stars. Few of them Chas recognized: Marlon Brando, James Dean on a motorcycle. To him it was a repellent muck-hole.
William Hughes, *Performance* (Tandem, London, 1970)

Patti Smith & Television – Live (1974)
'No other posters looked like mine,' says Richard
Hell. 'I didn't need to try to make them look
different, I just had different values than the other
bands, which at that time in New York were all
glitter and scarves and high heels and make-up.'

Design Richard Hell (Richard Hell) 11 x 17 inches,
43 x 28cm

In the winter of 1973–74 Sparks – a band centred on the Los Angeles-born Mael
brothers – were in a London studio recording what was to become *Kimono My
House*, their third album, and their first for Island Records. 'The vibes were great,'
remembers singer Russell Mael. 'We had Muff Winwood producing, the support
within the company was fantastic, we'd moved to England and this was our
dream: we were always Anglophiles.' Then they were informed that the energy
crisis was so extreme that recording would have to fit in with the scheduled
power cuts; it was no longer possible to assume that electricity would be
available when required. Worse was to come. A shortage of vinyl raised the very
real possibility that the album might not even be released (some of the leading
record companies had announced that they would be issuing no new product at
all in January 1974). As Mael notes dryly: 'It wasn't part of our dream of coming
to Britain.'

If Britain was running what was being compared to a Third-World economy, it
was only an exaggerated version of what was happening in all industrialized
nations. The comedown after the artificially engineered global boom of 1972–73
had been aggravated by the muscle-flexing of the oil-producing countries in the
Middle East, and even America found itself hit hard: although it had the cushion
of its own oil industry, domestic output hadn't grown since 1970, leaving all
growth in consumption (and, by extension, economic growth more generally)
dependent on imports. And when an oil embargo was followed by massive price
rises, the economy began to falter for the first time since the Second World War.
It was at this time that the term 'stagflation' was coined, to describe the deadly
combination of a slowdown in economic growth and rising inflation.

The recession in America didn't reach the same levels as it did in Britain, but
culturally it was possibly even more powerful; where the British economy had

been in decline since the devaluation of sterling in 1967, the crisis in the US abruptly challenged the promise of endless prosperity that had sustained the nation for three decades. Furthermore, the downturn coincided with defeat in Vietnam and with the growing Watergate scandal that was to force Richard Nixon to resign the Presidency in July 1974. For a country that had previously claimed ownership of the century, it was a triple blow: an assault on long-held assumptions about financial stability, military power and the integrity of the White House.

Within this picture, there were areas that were more profoundly affected than others, and most spectacular of all was the catastrophic financial collapse of New York City in the mid-'70s. Under Mayor John Lindsay (elected as a Republican in 1965 and then as a Liberal in 1969), the city had pursued what was in effect a Keynesian economic policy: raising taxes, creating government jobs and increasing welfare spending. The strategy had avoided many of the immediate problems of other cities, particularly serious race riots, but had also left New York vulnerable to recession in the national economy. By 1975 the city was on the brink of bankruptcy, and disaster was averted only by a massive Federal loan that would see it through to 1978: after that, the future was again uncertain.

And while the city's record on civil unrest was impressive, crime was slipping out of control: there was a three-fold increase in the murder rate in the space of a decade, and to the political right it seemed as though the horrors of hippydom were being compounded by the lawlessness of liberalism. The middle classes were fast losing faith with New York (in June 1975 it was reported that the upmarket Sovereign Building in Manhattan still had 285 of its 365 apartments available to rent, a year after completion), and even the government seemed to regard it as a latter-day city of the plains; President Ford's spokesman Ron Nessen famously compared it to a junkie daughter: 'You don't give her $100 a day to support her habit.'

The conflict with the right wing wasn't helped when one of the city's most famous sons, Andy Warhol, designed a poster for Democratic challenger George McGovern in the 1972 presidential elections. (Richard Nixon was returned with a landslide, taking forty-nine of the fifty states, including New York.)

Below

The Magic Tramps – Live (1972)
Fronted by Warhol 'superstar' Eric Emerson, the Magic Tramps relocated from LA to New York in 1971. Though they never signed a record deal, they were a live attraction locally and opened up the Mercer Arts Center to rock & roll; it was as support to the Magic Tramps that the New York Dolls first played the venue's Oscar Wilde Room, before starting their own residency there. 'It would be the Dolls in one room, Jonathan Richman in another, then us in another,' Suicide's Alan Vega remembered. 'Their room was like a party, ours was like a death scene.'

Amongst those who played in the Tramps at various points were Chris Stein and Ivan Kral, later of Blondie and Patti Smith Group respectively. Emerson left in 1974 and the following year was found dead on the decaying West Side Highway in New York. He had overdosed and, his body was left in the road, it was assumed in an unsuccessful attempt to look like an accident.

8.5 x 11inches, 58.5 x 39.5cm

Opposite

Suicide – *Suicide* (1977)
Artist Alan Vega and musician Martin Rev formed the duo Suicide after meeting in the late-'60s at the Project for Living Artists, an initiative funded by New York State – they made their live debut at the same venue. Confrontational from the outset, their early flyers from 1971–72 carried the slogan 'Punk music by Suicide' and the name itself was a challenge, though not as much as originally intended, as Vega later pointed out: 'I was reading a comic book called *Ghost Rider*, and one of the issues was called 'Satan Suicide'. I said, "That is it, let's just name the group Satan Suicide."'

The poster for their first album (advertised in the UK under the slogan 'Real rock & roll') took the design from the front cover and superimposed the photo of the band from the back of the sleeve: the dripping blood design was extended by cutting what would have been behind the photo and pasting it below.

Art Timothy Jackson & Alan Vega; photography Michael Robinson (Red Star)
15.5 x 23 inches, 58.5 x 39.5cm

ALBUM SUICIDE BY SUICIDE / BRON 508
SINGLE CHEREE BY SUICIDE / BRO 57

RED STAR RECORDS

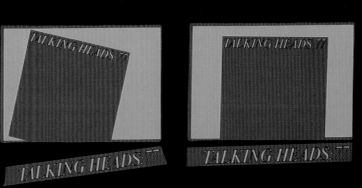

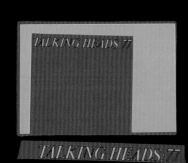

The city's decline was played out in the movies. Back in 1969 the Oscar-winning *Midnight Cowboy* had portrayed New York City as a corrupted, amoral world where the dreams of the '60s were dying in desperate loneliness. By the mid-'70s it was becoming possible to feel almost nostalgic for such an innocent cinematic vision, with films like *Death Wish* (1974) and *Taxi Driver* (1976) now showing a city trapped in a living nightmare, a society so wracked by crime that the only logical response would be to take up the gun. When Travis Bickle, played by Robert de Niro, comes to the conclusion that 'someone should just take this city and just flush it down the fucking toilet', it's little more than a restatement of the 1975 *New York Daily News* headline: 'Ford to City: Drop Dead'.

The complaint in *Death Wish* that 'decent people are going to have to work here and live somewhere else' was met politically by an alternative suggestion, that of 'planned shrinkage', as advocated by Roger Starr, a City housing official under Mayor Lindsay's successor, Abraham Beame. Starr called for a one-third reduction in the population of New York, to be achieved by the withdrawal of public support and services to neighbourhoods that were 'virtually dead'; the South Bronx, in particular, could, he argued, be turned into a national park, once the inhabitants had been removed. It wasn't a measure that was implemented – Starr was removed from office by Beame, and the city's population, though it did indeed shrink in the '70s, never did get back to the First World War levels for which he'd called – but the fact that the idea was even voiced suggested the desperation of the times. And in case the projected future wasn't entirely clear, the tagline to the 1981 movie *Escape From New York* spelt it out: '1997. New York City is now a maximum security prison'.

Opposite
Talking Heads – *77* (1977)
Perhaps the ultimate art-school band, the only member who did not study at Rhode Island School of Design was keyboardist Jerry Harrison, who had studied architecture at Harvard. The minimalist sleeve design for their first album was by David Byrne with assistance by Harrison, and was intended as a Day-Glo cover until they were told that Queens Litho, Sire's preferred printers, couldn't do it. 'We got on the phone and found a company that did polka records in the Midwest,' recalled Byrne. 'They said: Day-Glo? We'd be happy to do that. When Queens Litho heard that, they said they'd do it.'

Original sleeve design David Byrne; photography Mick Rock (Sire Records) 23 x 35 inches, 89 x 59cm

This political perception of New York as a pariah was mirrored within the music business. Before the Beatles, the city had been a key player in the industry, one of the hotbeds of doo-wop and girl groups, and home to the songwriting factory of the Brill Building, but in the wake of the British invasion, the balance of power had shifted. Once the folk boom had died down, the only successful groups to come out of New York in the late-'60s had been occasional, one-off acts like the (Young) Rascals and Vanilla Fudge. The more significant bands of the era, the Fugs and the Velvet Underground, had failed to get a national hearing, despite media attention and critical plaudits: peer-group acclaim counted for nothing in an America that was increasingly regarding New York as a cultural aberration.

The identification of the city with drugs, reflected in Nessen's comments, compounded the problem. The Velvet Underground had confirmed a nation's stereotype in 1967 when they sang not about a feel-good, spiritually enlightening, consciousness-raising drug, but instead about heroin. The following year, to make the point crystal clear, New York's most gifted rock & roll child, Frankie Lymon, overdosed, a dead junkie at the age of twenty-five. Even within rock's outlaw self-mythology, New York was considered to be a dangerous place. 'I lived in what's now called the East Village,' recalled Constance 'China' Burg of No-Wave band Mars; 'it was a place where the mob used to dump bodies, so just by exiting the house I would see gunshot victims all the time.'

In Britain it was seen differently. At around the time that New York was becoming known as 'the ungovernable city', the UK was earning the nickname 'the sick man of Europe' in honour of its moribund economy and its decaying urban fabric: there was, it appeared, an outcast status to be shared. And the remoteness that had informed British pop art still operated, radiating a golden glow of glamour; America was a semi-legendary place, a far-off land of which the British knew little but had heard much. In the States Lou Reed's tales of debauchery and drugged squalor may have been seen as documentaries; in Britain there was an element of vicarious depravity, a glam flirtation with the dark side.

The first British artist to register the influence of the Velvets had been David Bowie, whose 1967 song 'Little Toy Soldier' had quoted 'Venus In Furs' just months after its release. His

Wayne County & The Backstreet Boys

NEW SINGLE ON
max
RECORDS
ON SALE
NEXT WEEK!

IN PERSON AT
max's
SATURDAY AUG. 28
with WILLIE 'LOCO' ALEXANDER
and THE SCREWS

Shows At 10 And Midnight
213 PARK AVE. SOUTH AT 17th ST. 777-7870

Anton Perich prese

november 11th 10p

Right
Queen Elizabeth – Live (1972)
Above
Wayne County – 'Max's Kansas City' (1976)
Wayne, later Jayne, County had first met David Bowie as a cast member of the play *Pork*, which was staged at the Roundhouse, North London in 1971 (Leee Black Childers and Cherry Vanilla were also in the cast). Returning to New York, he formed the glam band Queen Elizabeth and subsequently signed to MainMan as a solo artist, though controversially nothing was released at any stage. The debut single did not come until 'Max's Kansas City', a tribute to the club where County had been the resident DJ for some years. 'People loved it because they got a name-check on it,' wrote County. 'Patti Smith was really thrilled: "Wow, that's the first time I've been mentioned in a song!"'

Right
8.5 x 14 inches, 35.5 x 21.5cm
Above
10.75 x 14.75 inches, 37.5 x 27cm

Cult Rock Posters

admiration for Reed's work had fuelled his fantasies of the New York underground, and when his management company, MainMan, opened an office in the city in the summer of 1972, he had – driven by his desire to emulate Andy Warhol and to acquire his own retinue of 'superstars' – recruited as many of the habitués of the art/rock hangout Max's Kansas City as he could find, including Cherry Vanilla, Wayne County and Leee Black Childers. The intention, apparently, was to acquire by association the divinely decadent credentials of the New York streets: Bowie might

have worn a 'man's dress', but everyone knew that he took it off when he got home; Wayne County, on the other hand, was prepared to take his/her transgender identity all the way to the operating theatre.

But Bowie, deceived by his long-distance love of Warhol and Reed, had misjudged the mood of America and, far from enhancing his reputation in the States, the New York connection probably did him more harm than good; the way to mass acceptance did not lie in playing up his bisexuality.

QUEEN ELIZABETH featuring WaYne County

the Wonder Woman with a host of performers in a saturday night dance & video

2am $2   The Kitchen 240 Mercer st

The truth was that New York acts had greater pulling power in Britain than they did in their own country.

The US poster issued to coincide with Reed's album *Transformer* told the story. On one side was a Lenny Bruce-styled photo of Reed, while on the back was a collection of articles culled, with one exception, from the British music press extolling him as a major figure in modern music; the only American piece was, tellingly, written for *Rolling Stone* by British photographer Mick Rock. The poster was aimed at the US industry and the implication was clear: this was an artist who was rated highly in Britain and was therefore worthy of attention. Similarly, the New York Dolls, the brightest hopes of American glam, made their British live debut supporting the Faces at what was then known as the Empire Pool Wembley, a 12,000-capacity venue that was a far cry from the clubs to which the then unsigned band were accustomed. The following year they got to play an even bigger venue at home, Madison Square Garden, but again only as support to a British act, this time Mott The Hoople.

Left

Lou Reed – Trade poster (1972)
Issued at the time of *Transformer*, this double-sided poster saw the reverse filled with articles extolling Reed's artistic status. The front included his own summary of his career to date.

This copy was donated by Jimi La Lumia, whose band the Psychotic Frogs were regulars at Max's Kansas City.

(RCA Records & Tapes)

Right

Tuff Darts – *Tuff Darts* (1978)
With their original line-up, Tuff Darts supported the New York Dolls and appeared on the 1976 *Live at CBGBs* album. Their own (and only) album came after the departure of singer Robert Gordon and his replacement by Tommy Frenzy. For the poster the cover-shot was presented in a torn design that was clearly intended to convey the spirit of punk.

This signed copy of the poster was originally owned by Greg Shaw, founder of the legendary Bomp! record label.

Art direction John Gillespie; photography Mick Rock (Sire Records) 23 x 35 inches, 89 x 58cm

A transatlantic trade route had been established whereby New York artists could acquire a reputation in Britain that might then give them sufficient status to take on the home market.

Partly this was due to the relative compactness of the UK industry. When the Dolls made their British TV debut performing on *The Old Grey Whistle Test* in 1973, presenter 'Whispering' Bob Harris may have sneered at them for being 'mock rock' (he'd already had a go at Alice Cooper and Roxy Music), but it was at least a national broadcast. And when Reed's single 'Walk On The Wild Side' was playlisted on BBC Radio One – which until 1979 shared much of its programming with Radio Two, including the afternoon show hosted by David Hamilton – it had an audience reach of nearly half the population.

But the really crucial factor in the British embrace of New York rock was the existence of the weekly music press. The oldest established music paper was *Melody Maker*, founded in 1926, but, despite proclaiming itself as 'the musicians' bible' and 'the thinking fan's paper', it had been overtaken in the '50s and '60s by its rival the *New Musical Express* (*NME*), which focused more fanatically on rock & roll and pop. The advent of underground rock in the late '60s saw both titles change direction and reap immediate dividends: the two papers saw a combined 50 per cent increase in sales in 1970–74. They were joined in 1970 by *Sounds*, while the existence of *Record Mirror* and *Disc* – both founded in the '50s and later to merge – meant that in the mid-'70s there were five nationally distributed weekly newspapers devoted to pop music. This was the golden age of British rock journalism, when competition to discover new talent was at its fiercest. A celebrated 1976 hate-piece on the *NME* in the *Sunday Times* magazine, describing the paper as being 'sloppy, self-indulgent, self-consciously hip', found space to outline the idealized *modus operandi* of the music press:

> The circle is tight. Recording artist 'has rap' with *NME* writer. Recording artist sells lots of records and gets famous. Music paper can claim to be thoroughly in touch because it carried substantial interview with famous star. The kids lap it up . . .

It may not always have worked so smoothly (*Record Mirror* predicted great things in 1972 for the bands Stud, Design and Byzantium, from all of whom we are still waiting to hear), but the ability of the weekly press in the '70s to set an agenda and to force a new band to the forefront of the industry's notice was unprecedented and unparalleled. And the legacy of British music from the '60s was sufficient to ensure that what was celebrated in the London-based media was taken seriously in America; hence that Lou Reed poster for *Transformer*. When Television's second album, *Adventure*, received unfavourable reviews in the weeklies, band leader Tom Verlaine dismissed his detractors: 'They aren't what I'd call writers,' he remarked, 'they're just sort of excitable personalities.' He may well have been right, but in the feverish atmosphere of the times, when each newspaper, each journalist was in pursuit of the next big thing, those excitable personalities exerted enormous power.

BLONDIE
NEW ALBUM NOW AVAILABLE ON RECORD & TAPE
also NEW SINGLE "IN THE FLESH"/"X OFFENDER"

PRIVATE STOCK
RECORDS, LTD.

Above

Punk #1

The cover of the first issue of *Punk* was drawn by John Holmstrom, who had studied at the School of Visual Arts in New York under comic legends Will Eisner and Harvey Kurtzman. Based on the studded jacket image from *Lou Reed Live* (this issue also featuring an article on Marlon Brando – who had fixed the rebel iconography of the biker jacket in *The Wild Ones* – and included adverts for shops where such garments could be bought), it helped fix the uniform of New York punks. In fact the black leather jacket became virtually synonymous with the city, at least until 1981 when the NYPD abandoned it in favour of less threatening lightweight blue jackets. The publication of the magazine was trailed with a fly-posting campaign that announced: 'Punk Is Coming!'

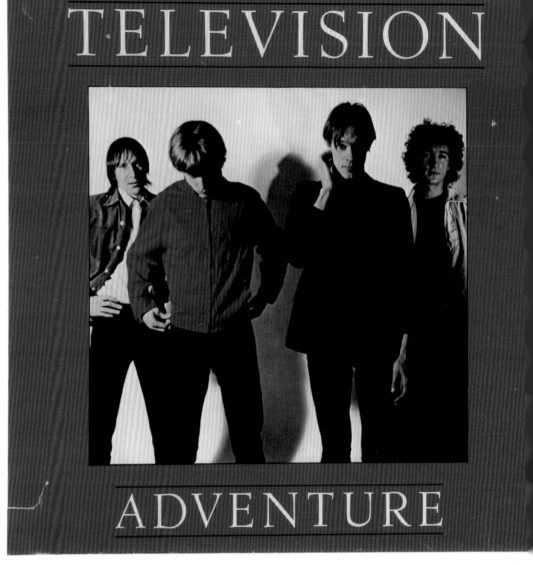

The career path that Lou Reed established, from New York to London and then back to a wider America, set a template for much of the decade, with the next generation of New York acts – Patti Smith, the Ramones, Television – finding a ready-made audience waiting in Britain, primed by an enthusiastic and sympathetic press. Not all made the final step to commercial acceptance in the States, but that such a development was possible was demonstrated by the case of Blondie.

Heavily championed by the British music press throughout 1977, and with Debbie Harry already becoming a ubiquitous poster presence, Blondie broke into the charts with the #2 hit 'Denis' that coincided with their third UK tour in early '78.

Later that year their third album, *Parallel Lines*, and particularly its accompanying single 'Heart of Glass' established them as a genuine worldwide success, giving them a #1 single at home. Significantly, it was produced by Mike Chapman, who – unlike most of his erstwhile protégés – had successfully made the transition away from glam.

These were bands who flourished in the space opened up by the New York Dolls. The Dolls themselves finally split in 1975, leaving behind two albums, a taste for management in the mind of London entrepreneur Malcolm McLaren (who had overseen their last days), and a fundamentally transformed musical landscape in New York. When the Dolls formed there was a dearth of live venues in the city; by the

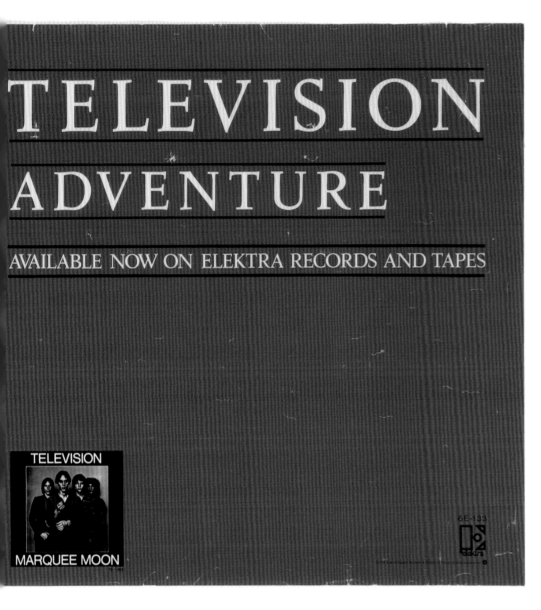

TELEVISION
ADVENTURE

AVAILABLE NOW ON ELEKTRA RECORDS AND TAPES

TELEVISION
MARQUEE MOON

6E-133

time of their demise, a circuit of clubs such as Max's Kansas City, the Bottom Line – where Suzi Quatro supported the Dolls in 1974 – and, most notably, CBGBs was flourishing. The result was a live music scene that in the middle years of the decade was undoubtedly the most exciting in the western world.

It was in this environment that the first issue of *Punk* magazine was launched in December 1975, giving a media-friendly name to what was effectively a disparate collection of groups rather than a single style. (Two months earlier the *New York Times* had written of superstar manqué Bruce Springsteen that 'he takes to the stage with the bravado of a punk in a pool hall'.) Even here, however, it was the impact

in London that was most pronounced: '*Punk* was in fact more widely distributed in England than in the States,' says cartoonist and co-founder John Holmstrom. 'We had a huge influence on the early punk scene there.' In mid-'76, as Patti Smith and the Ramones were making their London debuts, bank clerk Mark Perry published the first British fanzine, *Sniffin' Glue*, to be followed by an avalanche of titles of wildly varying quality and lifespans.

Sniffin' Glue differed from *Punk* in several key respects. Firstly, its subtitle (*& Other Rock & Roll Habits For Punks*) appropriated the word 'punk' to describe the fan, rather than the scene or the musician, thus laying the foundations for a youth cult; secondly, its tone of messy, amateur enthusiasm

Right and overleaf

Flyers for the Roxy Club, London (1977)
Reproduced on the first commercially available colour photocopier in London, the flyers for the Roxy are an exception to the monochrome ethic that dominated the period.

They were primarily the work of Barry Jones, who had studied at the Jacob Kramer College of Art in Leeds and had worked under designer Zandra Rhodes. 'I'm a northerner from a small village in County Durham,' he reflects, 'so magazines, comics and movies were always the magical world outside. I was heavily into Marvel comics, especially Spiderman, and I was really in love with mass production of an image or design (my favourite artist of that time being Andy Warhol – so obvious!).'

The influence of comics was also apparent in the work of acts as diverse as the Sensational Alex Harvey Band, Suicide, Kiss, the Ramones and David Bowie (the copy shop where these flyers were copied was in Heddon Street in London's West End, where the sleeve for *Ziggy Stardust* was photographed). 'I genuinely believed that it was an art movement we were in,' says Jones, 'not a let's-get-famous-and-make-lots-of-money thing. Silly me!'

Design Barry Jones (Roxy Club)

made no attempt at anything approaching normal journalistic standards; thirdly, and perhaps most importantly, its mode of production differed: where *Punk* had been printed, *Sniffin' Glue* was photocopied.

In New York, as Holmstrom points out, 'the paper-plate offset shops were an affordable, high-quality means of reproducing a few hundred black-and-white images'. Richard Hell's fly-posters for Television and later for the Voidoids were likewise printed: 'I would have them run off

photo-offset which wasn't really more expensive than photocopying but would allow me to have a higher fidelity photo reproduction (getting the half-tone screens of the photos cost a little extra).' In Britain, on the other hand, the arrival on the nation's high streets of photocopying bureaux in the mid-'70s undercut the cost of printing by a substantial margin, particularly on short runs, a fact that facilitated the production of punk propaganda.

The democratization of artwork that ensued was celebrated

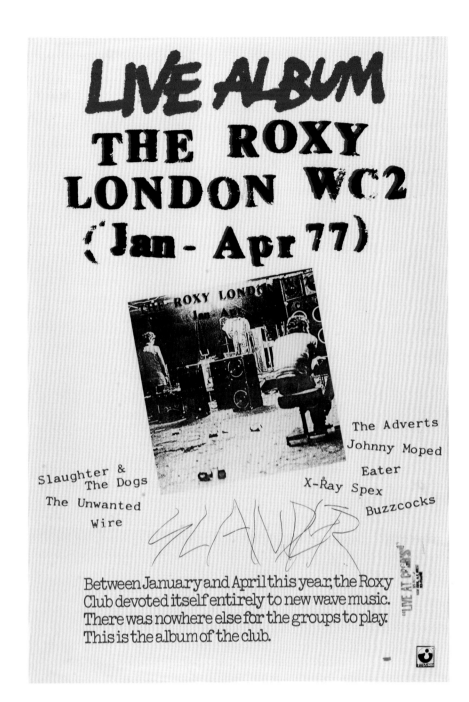

The Roxy was opened by promoters Andrew Czezowski and Susan Carrington on 1 January 1977; following a dispute over rent, their involvement ended just four and a half months later with a gig on St George's Day by Siouxsie & the Banshees.

The photograph on the sleeve of the posthumous album was taken after a Damned gig, when the ceiling tiles had been punched out by pogo-ers. (The 'Live at CBGBs' stamp and the graffito on this copy was presumably added by a member or fan of the band Slander.)

Design Barry Jones (Harvest Records) 20 x 30 inches, 76 x 50.5 cm

by Marco Perroni, guitarist with London band the Models and then with Adam & the Ants: 'You don't have to study graphics, you don't have to learn how to do airbrushing, you don't have to study printing, you don't have to go to art school. Get a newspaper, cut it up, stick bits of it to a piece of paper and take to the photocopier's.' The implications went beyond simple economics, helping to shape the imagery of the movement. 'Photocopying was cheap and it was clear,' Adam Ant argues, 'and it could also give you some interesting results with the quality of your artwork.'

The harsh tones produced by early photocopiers, as seen in *Sniffin' Glue* and on the posters and flyers made by the British bands, soon became recognizable as a new style. One further technical limitation also fed into the equation: 'There was never proper stage lighting at the punk clubs,' remembers photographer Jill Furmanovsky, 'so you had to use flash.' The result was a bleached-out, high-contrast image that was exaggerated by photocopying; from this was born the British punk aesthetic.

The Clash – Live (1977)
Adapted from the sleeve of the debut album, with an additional blank strip (complete with torn graphics) for gig details to be added.
Photographer Kate Simon was a friend of the Clash and was asked to take some shots of the band after a rehearsal in Camden Town. 'The shoot went very well,' she remembers. 'You know when things are going well and you've got a real opportunity and you're working with people you respect and love. Rarely did I find people that I believed in as much as I did with them, or people that were as photogenic as they were, and that knew how the process of photography works. They were great photo subjects. They were artists.'

Photography Kate Simon (CBS) 29 x 38 inches, 96.5 x 73.5cm

By April 1977, when the eponymous debut album by the Clash was released, the look of British punk was becoming established. So although the record was on CBS, a major label that had paid a handsome advance to secure the band, the sleeve was a deliberately downbeat affair featuring a heavily treated, high-contrast black-and-white photo of the band taken in Camden Lock, North London. 'I gave them a silver gelatin print,' remembers photographer Kate Simon, who took the shot. 'The record company took it and did a line print of it. They just did a treatment of it and the art director chose to do a line print. I thought it was great. What they did was original, no one had done that.' The sleeve, which style commentator Peter York described as 'the definitive interpretation of the new wave aesthetic', was hugely influential in determining that this was now a conscious decision rather than simply a low-budget acceptance of what was available.

SIDE 1:
THE NEXT BIG THING
I GOT YOU BABE
BACK TO AFRICA
MASTER RACE ROCK

SIDE 2:
TEENGENERATE
CALIFORNIA SUN
TWO TUB MAN
WEEKEND
(I LIVE FOR) CARS AND GIRLS

Bass, Lead Vocals, Tunes

Adny Shernoff: "I call the shots"

Lead Guitar, Vocals

Ross "The Boss" FUNichello: "To Me, Quantity is Quality"

Pacemaker Guitar

Top Ten: List his All-Time Top Ten

Percussion

Stu Boy King: "I don't make no mistakes Buddy Boy"

Producers: Murray Krugman and Sandy Pearlman
● The tag team champions pull another chestnut out of the fire . . . .

Recording Engineer: Tim Geelan

The Dictators – Reverse of LP sleeve for
Go Girl Crazy! (1975)
The debut Dictators album was the first product of the new generation of New York bands. The reverse of the sleeve showed the band members in their homes, surrounded by posters and magazine cuttings that illustrated their tastes: wrestlers, girls and rock & roll. 'The reason we had English glam posters up,' says bassist Andy Shernoff, 'was because that was what we liked at the time. . . there was no rock & roll in the US then.'

Photography David Gahr (Epic Records)

The urban setting of the Clash sleeve followed on from the first Ramones album, which had been released in May '76. For those who had never seen the band – that is, everybody save a handful of New York devotees – it was a startling artefact that unequivocally signalled a new era in rock & roll. Bryan Ferry's argument for 'a complete package' was here fully realized; from the shared surname, Ramone (taken from an early pseudonym of Paul McCartney, itself a knowing reference to rock history) to the group uniform to the intense conceptualization of the music, this was a band that presented a public face of absolute unity: it was impossible to imagine anything being added or taken away.

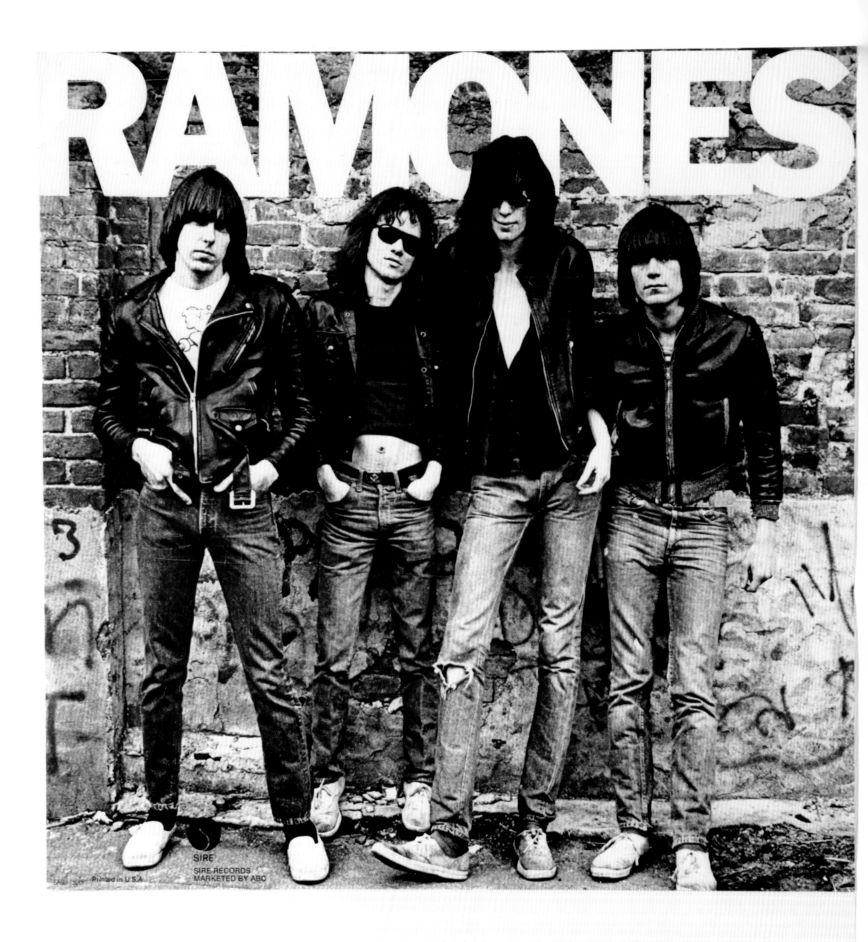

RAMONES

SIRE

SIRE RECORDS
MARKETED BY ABC

Printed in U.S.A.

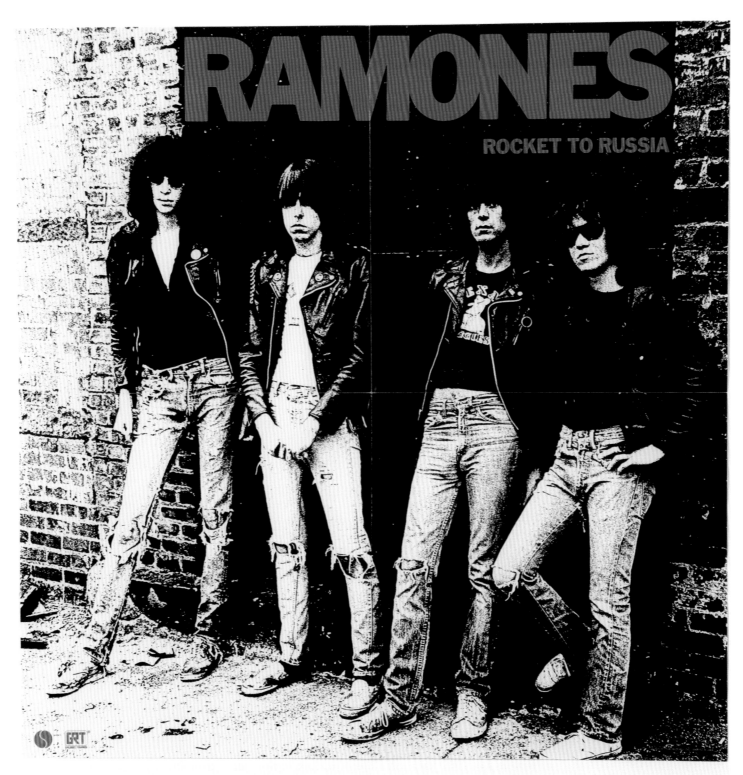

Left

Ramones – *Ramones* (1976)

Above

Ramones – *Rocket To Russia* (1977)

Photographer Roberta Bayley moved from London to New York in 1974: 'Everyone was broke, in both cities, it didn't seem like anything out of the ordinary. It was cheap to live a "bohemian" lifestyle in either city.'

This blank strip at the bottom of the debut album poster is perforated, so that it could be removed.

Left
Photography Roberta Bayley (Sire) 23 x 27 inches, 58.5 x 68.5cm
Above
Photography Danny Fields (Sire) 24 x 24 inches, 61 x 51cm

RAMONES

ROAD TO RUIN

Ramones – *Road to Ruin* (1978)
The fourth Ramones album was always intended to have a cartoon illustration on the cover, though the original drawing, by Glaswegian artist Gus Moorehead, had to be abandoned when there was a change in personnel. The version that was eventually used, complete with Marky Ramone, was by John Holmstrom.

The refusal to adapt the shape of the design for the medium of the poster leaves a massive empty space, in the same way that 12-inch singles by the band used only half an inch of playing surface, with the rest taken up by lead-off groove.

Design John Holmstrom (Sire) 23 x 35 inches, 89 x 59cm

The album effectively comprised a guide to the building blocks of New York popular culture. 'Listen To My Heart' is the entire output of girl group the Shangri-Las boiled down to an eight-line poem, '53rd and 3rd' revisits the male prostitution of *Midnight Cowboy*, and 'I Wanna Be Your Boyfriend' is the song that those who clocked into the Brill Building in the early '60s had always dreamt of writing. Meanwhile the clothes – zip-front black leather jackets, T-shirts, blue jeans – echoed the style of a 1950s street gang, as recently recreated in the 1974 cult movie *The Lords of Flatbush*. (Though the look came more directly from proto-punk band the Dictators: 'We didn't look good in satin and platforms, so we wore the same clothing onstage that we did on the street, which was sneakers, T-shirts, jeans and leather jackets,' recalls the Dictators' principal songwriter Andy Shernoff. 'The Ramones saw us playing at the Coventry, a glam club in Queens, and decided to borrow our look.')

It was as though, finding their city under attack from both within and without, the Ramones had chosen to respond by reclaiming their heritage in an attitude of defiant pride. The new elements – the rips in the jeans, the primitive instrumentation – located them in an era of decay, but the underlying themes were firmly rooted in traditional values.

For the sleeve of that first album, Sire Records commissioned a photographer whose work was promptly rejected by the band. In desperation they instead selected a shot that had been taken by Roberta Bayley for *Punk*. (Which, she explains, was why it was black and white: '*Punk* magazine didn't have colour photos in the beginning, so it never occurred to me to shoot colour.') The concept of a band being pictured in a city street was far from new; it had most famously been used by the Beatles on *Abbey Road*, but in that instance there was a sense of wonder that four of

the most famous men in the world should be seen in such prosaic surroundings, a feeling that they didn't truly belong there. With *The Ramones* there was no such doubt: they were not so much on the street as of the street. And unlike the sleeve of *Ziggy Stardust*, which had used colourization to add an alien quality to the urban textures, this was simple, unadorned and gritty.

In the autumn of the following year the band released their third album, *Rocket to Russia*. In the interim, little commercial headway had been made in the States, where the second album failed to do even as well as the first (despite an orthodox colour sleeve); but in Britain there was a more receptive audience, with a top-fifty placing for that record and a genuine hit single in the form of 'Sheena Is A Punk Rocker'. Unsurprisingly therefore, the emergent British punk vision made its impact on the new album. The sleeve photo, taken by Danny Fields, was a recreation of Bayley's shot: the four band members leaning against a brick wall in the streets near CBGBs. Again it was black-and-white, but this time the warm grey tones were replaced by a high-contrast treatment that echoed that of the Clash's first album. It was self-consciously punk – now that such a thing existed – and, while the clothes and the haircuts made no concession to the London scene, the presentation of the image certainly did.

It was one of the few occasions when British punk, a later movement, impacted upon the style of the original CBGBs generation. In general, the cultural traffic in 1976–77 was very definitely in the other direction, a fact that Richard Hell, amongst others, was keen to emphasize; as early as 1980 he was denouncing in the *East Village Eye* the historical revisionism that had elevated the British take on punk, and fiercely staking his city's claim to have invented the new music: 'The fact is that London punk was copied from New York punk in 1976.' While acknowledging the role played by the British media in covering the New York underground, he insisted that the sounds came from the Dolls and the look from the first incarnation of Television.

The key to that copying, Hell argued, was Malcolm McLaren. Inspired by his time in New York, McLaren had returned to Britain in 1975 with the intention of creating a band to walk through the valley of the shadow of the Dolls. He failed to persuade either guitarist Syl Sylvain or Hell himself to relocate to London as the front man for the project, but did take Hell's idea of a ripped T-shirt held together by safety-pins. These home-made individual pieces were redesigned, manufactured and transformed into items for sale in Sex, the boutique run by McLaren and Vivienne Westwood.

It was a move that typified the British relationship between clothes and subcultures. Ever since John Stephen opened the first of his shops in Carnaby Street in 1959, thereby helping to create the mod scene, boutiques had played a key role in the evolution of rock & roll style. In the early '70s Bowie, Bolan and Elton John had bought from places like Mr Fish, Mr Freedom and Granny Takes A Trip, when the New York Dolls were more likely to be picking up women's clothes from thrift shops and converting them at home: 'The same old New York thing of dressing like a tramp because you didn't have any money, but it became a style,' as Jayne County described it. Although Syl Sylvain and Billy Murcia of the Dolls had previously set up and sold a fashion design company specializing in 'a far out line' in sweaters, it was in Britain, appropriately for a nation of shopkeepers, that small-scale commerce and creativity were most closely linked; by the time of punk, the infrastructure was in place to exploit the commercial opportunities and spread the word beyond an immediate clique.

In short, London provided a platform, but it also proved itself adept at adaptation, at taking ideas originated in New York and translating them into something approaching mainstream success.

The ripped clothing pioneered by Hell was to become one of the classic statements of punk (celebrated implicitly in the title of the British fanzine *Ripped and Torn*), and helped shape the graphic design of the movement. It can be seen, for example, in the torn edges applied to Kate Simon's photo for the first Clash album sleeve, which were accentuated for the poster. And the poster advertising Hell's first UK tour, supporting the Clash, in 1977 made even more liberal use of rips, as well as employing the handwritten headlines familiar from the pages of *Sniffin' Glue*.

Hell, like the Ramones, had a pivotal influence on punk in both America and Britain, but there was a crucial additional factor in his work. The Ramones were at heart a New York band, paying tribute to its history in the same way as those other native New Yorkers, the Dolls had when they quoted the Shangri-Las ('When I say I'm in love. . .'), or doo-wop enthusiast Lou Reed, who in 1989 inducted the greatest of all the city's survivors, Dion DiMucci, into the Rock & Roll Hall of Fame. Hell, however, was an incomer: born in Kentucky in 1949, he moved to New York as a teenager. His take on the city was conditioned more by the enthusiasm of the convert than by the sense of being a part of an organic whole: where the ripped jeans of the Ramones suggested an attempt to hang on to the tattered remnants of a gang identity, his torn clothes reflected the immediate present of urban decline. When asked in 1978 why he hadn't accepted McLaren's invitation to move to London, his response displayed a neophyte's loyalty to a cause that, however desperate, was at least his own: 'We had started a scene in New York. New York was a central part of it, it was NY slum music.'

Right
Punk magazine - Awards Ceremony (1978)
The flyer for *Punk's* awards ceremony (screen-printed on textured card) includes a couple of surprising names. Kiss were emerging as the biggest band to come out of New York, with a blend of desexualized glam and heavy metal, but had earlier played on bills with the punk aristocracy; they went on to become the kings of merchandising, producing everything from bubblegum to a coffin (the Kiss Kasket), including perhaps more posters than any other act of the '70s. The presence of the Village People is much less explicable.

Design Bruce Carleton (*Punk*) 11 x 16.5 inches, 42.5 x 28cm

Overleaf - left
X-Ray Spex – 'Oh Bondage! Up Yours!' (1977)
The photo of Poly Styrene on the sleeve of X-Ray Spex's debut single was taken at the Roxy club. Poly: 'It was a black-and-white photo, and then I ran it through a colour Xerox, which it gives it that tone.'

Design Poly Styrene (Virgin) 20 x 30 inches, 76 x 50.5cm

Overleaf - right
X-Ray Spex – 'The Day the World Turned Day-Glo' (1978)
Poly Styrene: 'I got my boyfriend to photograph a globe we had at home, a black-and-white photo, and then I coloured it in with Stabilo felt-tips. And then I put it on Day-Glo green card – it was much more fluorescent originally.'

Artwork Poly Styrene (EMI) 20 x 30 inches, 76 x 50.5cm

You are cordially invited to attend the
1ST ANNUAL PUNK MAGAZINE AWARDS CEREMONY

THE MOST EXCITING EVENT OF THE YEAR! WE PROMISE!

PSSST! HEY SAILOR, GOIN' OUT?

B. Carleton

SCHEDULED TO APPEAR AND PRESENT AWARDS:
MEMBERS OF THE FOLLOWING FAMOUS ROCK GROUPS:

KISS **RAMONES**
BLONDIE **VILLAGE PEOPLE**
DEAD BOYS **DICTATORS**
RICHARD HELL + VOIDOIDS **AND INCREDIBLE SURPRISE GUESTS!**

PLUS LIVE ENTERTAINMENT!!
ROCK'N'ROLL- **SHRAPNEL!**
COMEDY- Romanoli's N.Y. SKITZ
CARTOONS- HOLMSTROM'S JOE SHOW
PLUS A SPECIAL CONCERT BY A SURPRISE ROCK'N'ROLL BAND!

YOU WILL...
★ MEET JOLLY- PUNK MAGAZINE'S NEW RESIDENT PUNK!
★ SEE THE **MUTANT MONSTER** LIVE AND IN PERSON!
★ LAUGH YOUR HEAD OFF!!
★ BE ABLE TO BUY DRINKS AT BAR.
★ NEVER FORGIVE YOURSELF IF YOU MISS THIS ONCE-IN-A-LIFETIME EVENT!

Tickets are:
5.50 IN ADVANCE
6.50 AT THE DOOR
GENERAL ADMISSION

FRIDAY THE THIRTEENTH OF OCTOBER · DOORS OPEN AT 7:00; SHOWTIME 8:00 PM
DOORS CLOSE 8:45

CLUB HOLLYWOOD
181 2ND AVE. (BETWEEN 11TH & 12TH ST.)

This is a High Class Affair!
DRESS APPROPRIATELY

FOR MORE INFORMATION, CALL:
226-7849 (PUNK MAGAZINE) AFTERNOONS
or
260-3314 (CLUB HOLLYWOOD) NIGHTS

CLUB HOLLYWOOD 181 2ND AVE
NEXT EMPIRE - 334 BOWERY
MANIC PANIC - 33 ST. MARKS PLACE
DEFIANT POSE - 5 ST. MARKS PLACE

TICKETS AVAILABLE AT THE FOLLOWING LOCATIONS!!!!
TRASH & VAUDEVILLE! - 4 ST. MARKS
REVENGE - 15 THIRD AVE
VILLAGE OLDIES - 170 BLEEKER ST.
MUSICAL MAZE - E 84TH ST.
DISCOPHILE - 26 WEST 8TH ST.

X ray Spex

I am a Cliche

Oh Bondage Up Yours!

THE DAY THE WORLD TURNED DAY-GLO
IAMA POSEUR

THE NEW SINGLE

WITH THE

VERTS

FIRST ALBUM

GARY
BORE

DAVID B
STA

The
double
from
1978 t
Out Now

RCA

4
IDENTITY

The instigators of punk are the same old petit-bourgeois art students, who a few months ago were David Bowie and Bryan Ferry look-alikes – who've read a little art history and adopted Dadaist typography and bad manners, and are now in the business of reproducing a fake street credibility.
Derek Jarman (diary entry, August 1976)

Say what you want, 'cos this is the new art school.
The Jam, 'Art School' (Paul Weller, 1977)

There was a demi-generation gap between American and British punk. Most of the key figures in New York (Debbie Harry, Patti Smith, Tom Verlaine, Richard Hell, Alan Vega) were born in the second half of the 1940s, their British counterparts nearly a decade later: John Lydon, Siouxsie Sioux, Paul Weller, Elvis Costello, Billy Idol, Dave Vanian. This was one of the major factors in the difference between the two subcultures, bringing to the relationship the impatience of the elder sibling and the noisy hero-worship of the younger, combined with fierce rivalry and the desire of each to eclipse the other.

Equally relevant were the respective backgrounds. Early American punk was rooted in what was predominantly a literary tradition, a tone set by English literature graduate Lou Reed with his stated intention to 'bring the sensitivities of the novel to rock music'. Patti Smith and Richard Hell were both published poets before they took up music, and the names adopted by Tom Verlaine and Cleveland band Pere Ubu (both derived from nineteenth-century French literature) left no doubt about their influences. 'It was a real reaction against disco music and the glitter-rock thing,' Patti Smith said of the CBGBs scene. 'Our lyrics were much more sophisticated and we weren't into artifice at all. The whole punk phenomenon in England was much more reactionary and more "high art".'

Her denial of glam is somewhat overstated: the sci-fi costumes and the facial glitter may have disappeared from the equation, but much of the underlying attitude and structure remained firmly in place. The Ramones, Wayne County and Cherry Vanilla all emerged from glam to find a place within punk, while the continued insistence on pseudonyms attested to the still powerful theme of make-believe, and Smith's own cross-dressing appearance on her debut album *Horses* (1975) suggested that gender issues hadn't entirely disappeared from the agenda. It's also notable that, just like glam, every major New York punk album came with a photo of the band on the sleeve, with the single exception of Talking Heads' *77*: the solipsistic allure of stardom was still alive and well.

And musically too there were parallels: the duo Suicide took rock reductionism even more seriously than did the Ramones, as heard on 'Ghost Rider' from their first self-titled album (1977). Based on a one-bar bass riff, its lyrics comprise little more than a stuttered set of catchphrases and

Above

Blondie – *Sunday Telegraph* (1978)
Photographed in the Gramercy Park Hotel, New York by Martyn Goddard (on a 500mm mirror lens), this news-stand poster is an indication of how rapidly Blondie were accepted by the mainstream of the British media.

Photography Martyn Goddard (*Sunday Telegraph*) 20 x 30 inches, 76 x 51cm buzzwords that evoked the primitive spirit of rock & roll: 'Ghost rider, motorcycle hero; baby, baby, baby, he's a-blazin' away like the stars, stars, stars in the universe.' If there was a precedent for this, it was Gary Glitter's 'Rock & Roll (Part 2)', not so much an instrumental as a rhythm-track accompanied by the occasional chanting of the phrase 'Hey! Rock & roll!'

It was certainly true, however, that the influence of glam took a slightly different course in Britain. The age difference meant that British punks were more likely to have grown up as fans of the genre, influenced by its promise of freedom through art and artifice, as Marco Perroni points out: 'We had the glam hangover, we were all old glam rockers, we weren't dole queue kids desperately trying to get a job. That whole thing about "Career Opportunities" and trying to get a job: we didn't want a job. Doing what? Because we came from Bowie and Roxy Music.'

Despite the imagery that became associated with punk – teenage unemployment, tower blocks, street-fighting youth – the most creative wing of the movement had little truck with such straightforward social realism: 'I hated all that dole queue shit,' says Adam Ant. 'I thought it was boring.' Instead, as he suggests, the enemy was identified as the slightly vague condition of 'boredom', against which were ranged the familiar weapons of glam: primarily, an emphasis on the self-created fantasy image of the individual. The wardrobe may have changed, but the desire to dress up was every bit as pronounced. The first wave of British punks was just as dedicated to the notion of stardom as Bolan had ever been, and the Kinks' slogan that 'everybody's in showbiz, everybody's a star' was extended to include even the audience, so that when the Sex Pistols made their notorious 1976 TV appearance with Bill Grundy, they were accompanied by four hardcore fans, members of what was already being celebrated in the music press as the Bromley Contingent.

So closely were the two styles allied that when punk bands got into the recording studios, they returned to the anthems of the preceding generation: Siouxsie & the Banshees covered T. Rex's '20th Century Boy', the Skids addressed Mott The Hoople's 'All The Young Dudes' and Eater converted Alice Cooper's 'I'm Eighteen' into a more age-appropriate 'Fifteen'. Similarly, a number of punks chose as producers the backroom boys who had made glam: Chris

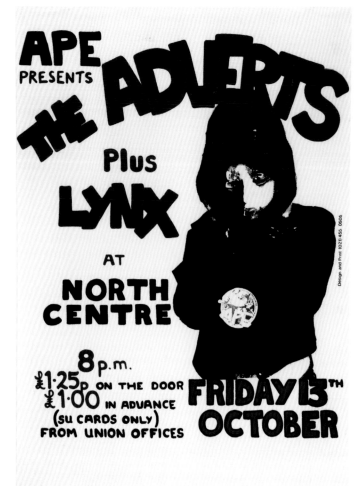

Above

The Adverts – Live (1978)
A screen print using an unusual and subtle two-colour mix of chocolate-brown and black.

18 x 25 inches, 64 x 45cm

Right

Richard Hell & the Voidoids – UK tour (1977)
Richard Hell was unimpressed by a poster that seemed more appropriate to a Hammer movie than to an art-punk band: 'At the time the poster seriously annoyed me. It's interesting just as an artefact of the record companies' mentality and their shaky take on what the bands were doing, but it's still dumb as shit.'
   This copy was formerly owned by Voidoids guitarist, Robert Quine (1942–2004), probably the most creative musician in the New York punk scene. He was said to have disliked the ripped clothing that was the group's trademark, and by the second album was photographed wearing a shirt and sports jacket.

(Sire Records) 19.5 x 28 inches, 71 x 50cm

Thomas went from working with Roxy Music to producing the Pistols, Phil Wainman from the Sweet to Generation X, Guy Stevens from Mott The Hoople to the Clash (as well as Mike Chapman's production of Blondie). It was a lineage that did not go unremarked even at the time: 'Some bloke came up to me the other day,' Adam noted in 1977, 'and said: "It's glam rock."' He was right.

In addition, glam donated the melodrama of imminent apocalypse. Bowie had announced in 1972 that the end of the world was nigh ('Five years, that's all we got'), had confirmed in the parenthetical dating of 'Aladdin Sane (1913–1938–197?)' that we were on the brink of world war, and had then shown us a post-holocaust world on *Diamond Dogs* ('as the last few corpses lay rotting on the slimy thoroughfare...'). It turned out to be scare-mongering – the world was still turning at the end of the decade – but it was a seductive image in a society that seemed in danger of terminal collapse. With civil war raging in Northern Ireland, with the last card of the Empire being played out in Rhodesia, and with the worst ever industrial relations, Ted Heath had called a general election in February 1974 on the theme of 'who governs the country?' To which the country's response had been equivocal at best. For the first time, union power looked, and had proved, capable of bringing down an elected government, and Bowie wasn't the only one to predict that the nation was facing a terminal crisis, and that normal rules no longer applied: James Herbert's best-selling horror novel *The Rats* (1974) depicted a sleazy, wounded Britain fighting for survival against the ultimate urban nightmare, while the 1972 paperback of George Shipway's populist thriller *The Chilian Club* was happy to ask rhetorically: 'Don't you ever feel like shooting a Union Leader?'

The increasingly confrontational tone of society was picked up in rock & roll, with the *Melody Maker* in July 1976, on the very eve of punk, denouncing the Doctors of Madness and the Heavy Metal Kids, fronted by Gary Holton, for 'inciting the audience to violence'. Two years earlier, in the *NME*, Alex Harvey had predicted precisely this turn of events: 'Someone's got to come along and say: fuck you,' he announced in condemnation of the existing order of things. The Sex Pistols proceeded to do just that, inciting violence with apparent glee and taunting society with apocalyptic self-images: 'We're the future, *your* future...'

Also influencing the evolution of British punk was the apparently alien tradition of pub rock. Initially seen as a reaction against the excesses of both the corporate stadium bands and glam, the London pub rock scene – in the form of Ducks Deluxe, Brinsley Schwarz, Chilli Willi & the Red Hot Peppers and others – had gone back to the less showy roots of rock & roll, offering an easygoing blend of country and r&b with a strong emphasis on traditional virtues. Despite the 1974 appearance in the top 20 of Ace's single 'How Long', there was little indication that this was ever going to trouble anyone save the regulars at the Tally Ho in Kentish Town, until a second, more aggressive generation emerged from the live circuit that pub rock had opened up. Chief amongst them were Dr Feelgood, offering a psychotic reaction to r&b and adopting a lean and hungry look ('We didn't set out to look like deranged bank clerks,' protested singer Lee Brilleaux),

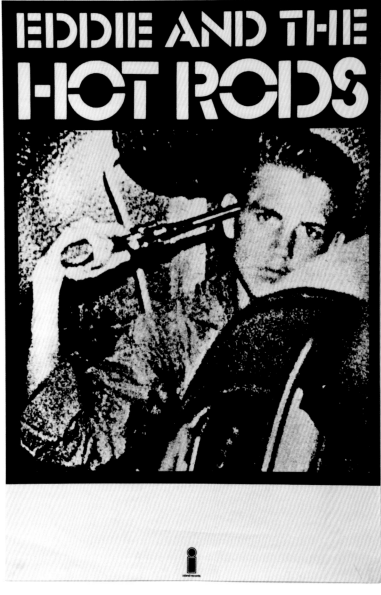

Above

Dr Feelgood – *Malpractice* (1975)

In 1977 the *NME Encyclopaedia of Rock* said of Dr Feelgood: 'Formed 1971 in Canvey Island, Essex – a small, eyesore oil-refinery community in Thames estuary that might be described as the arm-pit of South East England.' Their second album, *Malpractice*, was released in stereo – unlike the debut – but that was as far as the compromises went: the sleeve reflected the stripped-down, no-frills threat of the music. Keith Morris's photo of four guys who look like they could have been the villains in an episode of *The Sweeney* exudes a brutal realism; there's no artifice, no stylistic involvement here. The band's logo can be seen in the window of the barber shop

Photography Keith Morris (United Artists)

Above

Eddie & the Hot Rods – *Live* (1976)

The sleeve for the Rods's single 'Wooly Bully' (June 1976) was based on a photograph found in *True Detective* magazine, showing an American youth who'd been dumped by his girlfriend and was threatening to kill himself. The same image was used for gig posters and on the 1977 debut album *Teenage Depression* though for the latter, at the insistence of the record company, it was colourized.

The font is based on Glaser Stencil Bold by Letraset, amended by designer Michael Beal: 'I liked tweaking everything, so everything was original or new. Basically it was me working to impress typesetters or to impress photographers, because I thought if you can do that, you can intrigue people who don't know what any of this stuff is about.'

Design Michael Beal (Island) 20 x 30 inches, 76 x 51cm

Ultravox – Live (1977)

The second Ultravox album *Ha! Ha! Ha!* (still with original singer John Foxx, who had studied at the Royal College of Art) came with a sleeve whose repeated photos echoed Warhol, while the quality of the photographic representation clearly derived from the Xerox culture of punk. The poster for the accompanying gigs extended the image by the insertion of a blank strip.

(Island Records) 28 x 39 inches, 100 x 71cm

Above

Iggy Pop – Live (1978)

This live poster was based on a photo from the inside sleeve of the album *TV Eye Live*.

Photography Este; original album art direction Barney Wan (International Concert Organization) 25 x 35 inches, 90 x 64cm

IGGY
Pop
RCA

LUST FOR LIFE
PL 12488

TV EYE LIVE
PL 12796

THE IDIOT
PL 12275

Drums
SCOTT ASHTON
Bass
GARY RASMUSSEN
Guitar
FRED (SONIC) SMITH
Keyboards, Guitar, Harmonica
SCOTT THURSTON

Iggy Pop – Poster mag (1978)
This is the reverse of a double-sided poster that
folds out from an A4 tour programme. The font is
taken from the 1978 album *TV Eye Live*, the album
that the tour was promoting.

(RCA Records & Tapes) 23.5 x 33 inches, 60 x 84cm

Identity

"HEROES" DAVID BOWIE

Tomorrow Belongs To Those Who Can Hear It Coming

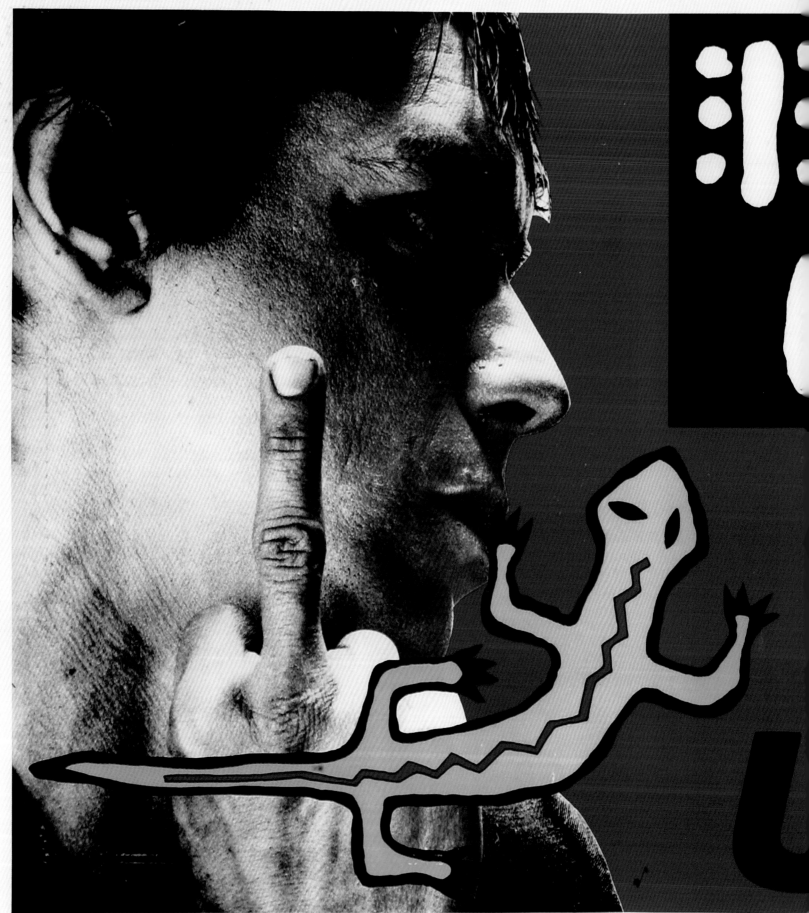

David Bowie *"Heroes"* (1977)
Iggy Pop – *The Idiot* (1977)
The poses on both album sleeves were derived
from the painting 'Roquairol' by the German
expressionist Erich Heckel. The slogan 'Tomorrow
belongs to those who hear it coming' was one of
a number used by RCA at the time (including
'There's old wave, there's new wave, and there's
David Bowie') and subsequently appeared on the
poster promoting *Peter and the Wolf* (p. 57)

Previous page - left
Photography Sukita (RCA Records & Tapes) 24 x
17 inches, 61 x 43cm
Previous page - right
Photography Keith Morris (United Artists)

Left

Iggy Pop - USA 1979 (1979)
**A poster bought at a merchandise stall at a 1979
Iggy gig.**

Design Iggy Pop (James Osterberg) 38 x 25 inches,
63.5 x 96cm

Identity

107

PERE UBU

New Album
'DUB HOUSING'
CHR 1207

Appearing at

and their successors, Eddie & the Hot Rods, whose roots in
'60s garage music made them either the last pub rock band
or the first punk band, depending on one's perspective. In
either event, they demonstrated that it was possible to force
entry into the business from outside. 'We weren't one of
those cultured groups that came up being nurtured into the
music industry,' points out singer Barrie Masters – and
thence into the charts.

Perhaps more influential still were Kilburn & the High Roads,
a curious, motley collection of musicians, fronted by Ian

Dury and performing his equally curious and motley repertoire of songs. They made no commercial impression at the time, but their final gig, as Ian Dury & the Kilburns in June 1976, saw them supported by the Stranglers and by a new band called the Sex Pistols. During the latter's set, Dury noted that the singer looked familiar: 'He had the safety-pin, and was leaning forwards and growling and holding the microphone just like I did.' As Dury pointed out to the group's manager, Malcolm McLaren: 'He's copying me isn't he?'

Above

Iggy Pop & James Williamson – *Kill City* (1977)
The release of demos made by Iggy with guitarist James Williamson in the wake of the Stooges's split was accompanied by a poster that unusually didn't include a photo of the man himself.

(Radar Records) 20 x 30 inches, 77 x 52cm

STIFF RECORDS.
WHERE TASTE IS NOT A PROBLEM.
HE DOES IT
IN PUBLIC.
IAN DURY
NEW BOOTS
AND
PANTIES!!
STF 0002
MANUFACTURED
AND DISTRIBUTED
BY ARISTA RECORDS
© 1978 Stiff Records, Ltd.

Previous pages and left

Ian Dury – *New Boots and Panties* (1977–78)
Barney Bubbles was the pseudonym of designer Colin Fulcher (1942–83). In the 1960s he was the lighting engineer at the UFO Club, and subsequently worked closely with Hawkwind. His best-known work, though, came at Stiff Records in the second half of the '70s, when he brought his knowledge of twentieth-century art and design – particularly futurism and constructivism – to bear on his work.

In late 1977 Jake Riviera left Stiff, the label he had co-founded, to create Radar Records and took with him Elvis Costello and Nick Lowe. With Ian Dury the only potential star left on Stiff, the company began a major (and successful) promotion of his debut album, hence the multiplicity of posters. 'He does it in public' was part of the US promotion for the album.

Design Barney Bubbles (Stiff)
Previous pages
both 20 x 30 inches, 76 x 50.5cm
Left
24 x 30 inches, 91.5 x 61cm

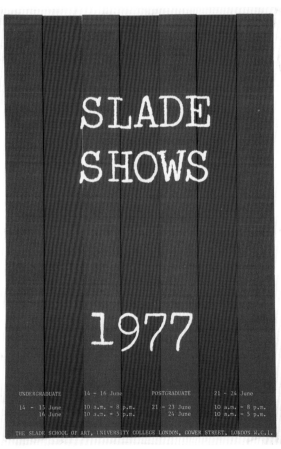

Above

Slade Art School - end of year show (1977)
The influence art schools had on the aesthetics of rock & roll, the way they shaped the visual style of the '70s, eventually and inevitably fed back into the original institutions. This poster, created by students at the Slade Art School, is perfectly in keeping with its period, resembling a new wave album promotion.

20 x 30 inches, 76 x 51cm

Despite these very specific influences, perhaps the key difference between British punk and the American incarnation was the former's association with the art school tradition. It wasn't a new relationship within rock & roll. The overt connection with the art world had peaked in the late '60s with the drugs bust of Mick Jagger alongside art dealer Robert 'Groovy Bob' Fraser, an event commemorated in Richard Hamilton's series of six silkscreen paintings 'Swingeing London '67', based on a photograph of the two men handcuffed together in the back of a police car. But despite the art school education of '60s rock stars like John Lennon, Keith Richards, Pete Townshend and Ray Davies, the curious fact is that none pursued the practice of visual art. ('I did try for one job with my little portfolio,' recalled Richards, 'and I was promptly turned down.') The background informed their thought and their approach to music – particularly Townshend, who applied the theories of auto-destructive art propounded by Gustav Metzger, a visiting lecturer while he was a student, to his stagecraft – but only Ron Wood took up art even as a sideline; the principal rock star of that generation who did become involved in the art world was, paradoxically, David Bowie, who had no formal training.

The '70s, on the other hand, saw a musical flourishing of ex-students with a more acute sense of the possibilities of modern art. To a large extent, this was a natural evolution. In the late '50s the faculties of British art schools – particularly those outside the prestigious London institutions – hadn't always been receptive to the encroachment of popular culture, but as the more adventurous students of that time became the new establishment, the atmosphere gradually changed; by the time Ian Dury, a student at Walthamstow School of Art, encountered a new teacher in the shape of Peter Blake, things were far freer, as Dury later recalled:

'Do you like rock & roll?' he asked.
'Yes.'
'Boxing and wrestling?'
'Yes, and tits and bums, gangsters, teddy boys, Jayne Mansfield and Marlon Brando.'
'Then why don't you paint pictures of what you like?'
Dury went on to become both a practising artist and even a lecturer before turning to rock & roll, the first to make the jump from the art school common room to the *Top of the Pops* green room.

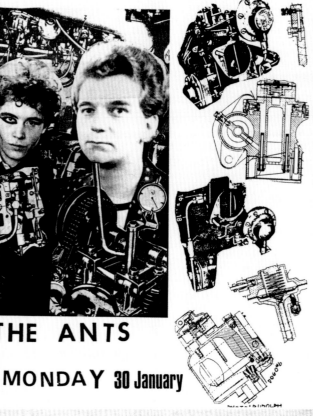

ADAM AND THE ANTS
at the 1001 CLUB MONDAY 30 January

Other pop artists also made an impact on the next generation of rock stars: Adam Ant studied under ephemera-obsessed Eduardo Paolozzi ('he was the governor; fucking brilliant'), and Bryan Ferry under Richard Hamilton. Indeed Hamilton's famous 1957 definition of pop – 'popular (designed for a mass audience), transient (short-term-solution), expendable (easily forgotten), low-cost, mass-produced, young (aimed at youth), witty, sexy, gimmicky, glamorous, big business' – could have been written twenty-five years later as a description of Roxy Music and glam, though few could have predicted at either time just how durable the products were to become.

Ferry made his debt explicit: 'I found it was like pop art,' he said of his songwriting. 'I was using images, throwaway clichés and amusing phrases that you found in magazines or used in everyday speech – stylistic juxtapositions.' The first Roxy Music single, 'Virginia Plain', shared its title with a 1964 painting he had made, based on a billboard poster, while he named his 1978 solo album *The Bride Stripped Bare* in tribute to Marcel Duchamp's *magnum opus* 'The Bride Stripped Bare by Her Bachelors, Even' (Hamilton had curated Britain's first Duchamp retrospective at the Tate Gallery in 1966).

By the time of punk, modern art had thoroughly permeated rock & roll. Adam Ant, for example, drew freely on the imagery of Allen Jones's fetishistic depictions of sado-masochism, on the violence of Marinetti and the Futurists, and on the photomontage techniques of John Heartfield: 'He really had some balls to take on the Nazis and just take the piss out of them. I just thought this was a really excellent way of de-bollocking the fascist thing; it was very brave, very courageous.' Heartfield, a German Dadaist who had been born Helmut Herzfeld and anglicized his name in protest at the First World War, was also to inspire the Siouxsie & the Banshees 1979 single 'Mittageisen (Metal Postcard)', at a point when punk had rejected its early use of Nazi symbolism and was firmly aligning itself with the anti-fascist movement.

'This "new wave" has got to take in everything, including posters, record-covers, stage presentation, the lot,' announced Mark Perry in *Sniffin' Glue* in September 1976 and because, even more than the '60s generation, punk was populated by ex-art school students, his call was heeded: the opportunities offered by photocopying to produce posters, flyers and singles sleeves for independently released records were eagerly seized upon by bands

throughout Britain. Characteristic of the era was Spizz; a glam fan who had studied art at Solihull College of Technology, he subsequently turned down a place at Bath Academy of Art when, inspired by a Clash gig at Barbarella's in Birmingham, he decided to take up performing instead. His bands (the variously named Spizz Oil, Spizzenergi, Athletico Spizz 80, Spizzles) used posters and artwork designed by him, the best known of which was a photo of William Shatner that adorned 'Where's Captain Kirk?', the first ever #1 in the indie charts when they were launched in January 1980. Photocopied and then painted over, it had the atmosphere of a screen print and was, as Spizz says, 'something Warholesque'.

He wasn't the only one to make the connection. 'If punk graphics came from anywhere,' says graphic designer Michael Beal, who worked with Eddie & the Hot Rods, Johnny Thunders and the Only Ones, 'the thing you would trace it back to was Warhol's screen printing. That was in the back of your mind. Looking cheap and put-together, not glossy and airbrushed.' Poly Styrene of X-Ray Spex agrees: 'If I had a subconscious inspiration, it would have been Andy Warhol's Campbell soup tins: everyday consumer objects.'

Above

Adam & the Ants – Gig flyers (1977?)
'Let's get together before it's too late, collect up the ideas, duplicate,' sang Adam Ant on his 1979 single 'Zerox', and no other punk artist made better use of the technology. The flyers he produced for Ants gigs in the '70s are carefully considered collages that reflect influences from sources as diverse as Allen Jones (far right), Magritte and Duchamp (centre right) and Eduardo Paolozzi (far left). 'I was aware that they were collectable,' he says, 'and I was aware that I could use my art-school training to do something a bit more interesting, a bit more thoughtful. It wasn't really the images that anyone else was using. With punk, the whole idea was to shock, the idea of taking recent history that we'd all grown up with, because we were the baby-boomers, and not hiding from it but turning it upside down.'

Design Adam Ant (Adam Ant) A4

Warhol's 1960s silkscreen prints of the icons of American mass-culture from Marilyn Monroe and Elvis Presley to Coca-Cola bottles and the FBI's most wanted criminals ('I adore America and these are some comments on it,' he said in 1960) were the best-known products of pop. Initially seen as objects of industrial mass-production, his repeated images had acquired an almost charming hand-made quality by the 1970s, so rapidly had art and technology moved on. But the impact of a single image reiterated with minimal, if any, variations continued to resonate: it can be seen, for example, on the cover of Eno's *Taking Tiger Mountain* (*By Strategy*) (1974) and on the poster for Lou Reed's *Coney Island Baby* (1976). 'When the paintings are continuously strung along a wall space,' wrote critic John Coplans, 'the pervasively rhythmic repetition of the imagery becomes a metaphor of rock & roll's powerful incessant beat, the fragmented overprinted images suggesting optical after-images caused by stroboscopic light.'

Having designed album covers for jazz acts, including Count Basie, when he was a commercial artist in the '50s, Warhol went on to become the artist most closely identified with rock & roll. His direct association started with his patronage of the Velvet Underground (and his painting for the cover of their 1967 debut album) and reached fruition when the Rolling Stones – perhaps goaded by the Beatles' choice of Blake and Hamilton to design consecutive album sleeves – commissioned him to create the cover of *Sticky Fingers* (1971). By the end of that year, Bowie was visiting him in New York and playing him the acetate of a new song titled simply 'Andy Warhol'. Ferry too, amongst whose lecturers had been one of Warhol's associates Mark Lancaster, cited him as an influence.

And even as punk was rediscovering his '60s work, Warhol was returning to his collaboration with the Stones, creating the sleeve for *Love You Live* (1977). Having produced a series of prints of Jagger two years earlier, he now created a collaged silkscreen with ripped paper strips that had been painted and drawn upon, a technique that made perfect sense in the context of punk.

Emerging as the most famous pop artist of all, possibly the most recognizable painter in the world, Warhol spent much of the '70s celebrating his fame and that of the aristocratic showbiz circles in which he could now move. His most influential years behind him, he now became an even more

prominent figure, pursuing stardom and asserting: 'If you want to know all about Andy Warhol, just look at the surface of my paintings and films and me, and there I am. There's nothing behind it.' It was a pose and/or creed that was lost on neither glam nor punk.

Above

Cherry Vanilla Band – Live (1978)
A confused design for this Dutch gig poster, but one whose jumble of typefaces prefigures a style that was to become more common in the following decade.

16.5 x 23.5 inches, 60 x 41.5cm

In *24 Hour Party People* (2002), the movie account of Factory Records in Manchester, the label's founder, Tony Wilson (played by Steve Coogan) is seen emerging from an early Sex Pistols gig and ripping down a poster of Bowie in symbolic rejection of what has gone before. There was a cinematic precedent for the gesture – Wes Craven's horror classic *The Hills Have Eyes* (1977) had included in shot a torn poster for *Jaws* (1975), to indicate that we had now reached a new level of terror; to which *The Evil Dead* (1981) had responded by showing a torn poster of *The Hills Have Eyes*, (and Craven in *A Nightmare on Elm Street* had . . .) – but in this context it was intended to be indicative both of the desire to claim a brand-new start for rock and of the central importance of posters.

The former was, given the range of influences that bore down upon punk, an exaggeration, but the latter was a simple statement of fact. Largely excluded from television and from daytime radio, punk had to struggle to make its voice heard and, outside the pages of the British music press, the most effective way was through posters. Fortunately the availability of photocopying and print shops made the production of posters achievable on a near-zero budget for a newly formed band. 'People posted flyers because it was the only advertising anyone could afford,' says Richard Hell, while Adam Ant remembered the amateur ethos of the period: 'Anyone that could get us a poster on the street was a manager in those days.'

And even for those with a record deal, it remained a vital form of communication, with Hell continuing to make his own gig-posters into the late '70s: 'Sire's promotion sucked and had nothing to do with us, and anyway they didn't contribute anything to local gigs.' Michael Beal, who had worked with Eddie & the Hot Rods from an early stage, found the same situation when the band signed to Island Records: 'I thought: this company does great sleeves – Sparks, Roxy – just quality. And then when we got there, it was another story entirely. They didn't like us, we were just oiks from Southend. We weren't cool like Bryan Ferry. It was fun though; made for good battles.' Similarly Poly Styrene struggled to maintain her original vision when confronted by an in-house art department: 'We had a real fight with EMI to use my artwork. They thought it was way too stroppy. They introduced me to a really good artist who did sepia – really, really classy – but I didn't think it was right for my

generation. So I had a little bit of a battle with them, but then they kept my artwork.'

It was a situation common to a generation of bands that, for the first time in rock history, turned up at record company offices complete with a fully realized graphic and visual style, courtesy more often than not of an art school graduate who was a member, or at least a friend, of the group.

The one band who could (eventually) count on record company support were the Sex Pistols, who signed to Richard Branson's Virgin label in May 1977, having previously been dropped from the rosters at EMI and A&M.

Above

The *Sun* – news-stand poster (1977)
After some initial confusion over whether punk was a joke or a threat ('Punk Rock is the craziest pop cult of them all,' said the *Sun* in October 1976), the tabloids soon decided that denunciation was the best option.

Right
Sex Pistols - 'Anarchy in the UK' (1976)
One of the most startling and iconic images to
emerge from punk, Jamie Reid's poster for the
first Sex Pistols single was created from a 4 x 8
inches fabric souvenir flag photographed by Ray
Stevenson. The combination of the shredded
symbol of Empire and the blackmail typeface was
to be hugely influential and to suggest a political
dimension to the new movement.

Design Jamie Reid, photography Ray Stevenson
(EMI) 28 x 38 inches, 96.5 x 71cm

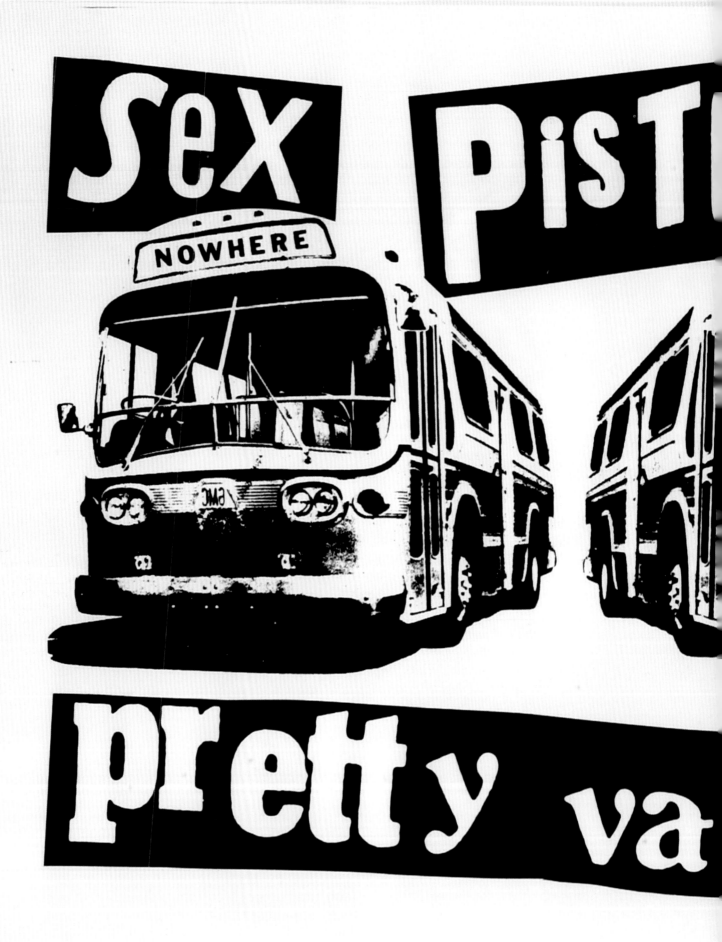

: NEW SINGLE ON VIRGIN RECORDS VS

Left

Sex Pistols - 'Pretty Vacant' (1977)
Jamie Reid's image of two buses – originally with
'Nowhere' written as the destination for both –
was first printed as a poster in 1972 by Suburban
Press (the organization that Reid was part of in
London), and picked up the Situationist magazine
Point Blank in San Francisco the following year for
a pamphlet about city transit policy. It appeared
again on the Sex Pistols' *Anarchy* newspaper in
'76 and, in its final form (with 'Nowhere' and
'Boredom' as the destinations) on the back of the
picture sleeve for the 'Pretty Vacant' single.

Design Jamie Reid (Virgin Records) 28 x 38 inches,
96.5 x 71cm

Overleaf

**These High Street poster magazines made it
absolutely clear that, despite the official Sex
Pistols artwork, the real star of punk was Johnny
Rotten.**

Clockwise from top left: *Punk* (Byblos Productions,
1977) printed by Varnicote, Worcestershire; *New
Wave* (Choice Publishing, 1977) editor Vic Lime,
layout Michele Mortimer; *Sex Pistols* (Pepperwell
Ltd, London E11, 1977); *Total Punk!* (1977)

Judged purely by column inches, they were undoubtedly the biggest act in Britain that year, but they also faced the most concerted policy of exclusion from the mainstream media. Excoriated by the press, banned from advertising – let alone appearing – on radio and television, and with a blanket broadcast prohibition on their #1 single 'God Save The Queen' that prevented even punk-friendly DJ John Peel from playing the record, the recourse to posters was still more necessary. They were one of the few groups ever who regularly posed for publicity photos alongside their latest poster.

Almost uniquely among major punk acts, however, the Pistols' artwork itself never featured images of the band; 'The Sex Pistols was a work of art,' Fred Vermorel, one of Malcolm McLaren's associates, was later to declare, but it wasn't a work that was to be conventionally exhibited. Instead McLaren broke with the glam tradition to allow Jamie Reid, his colleague from art student days, to explore what was effectively an iconoclastic anti-pop style. Despite the two men's insistence that the visual presentation of the group was derived from the obscure European art movement, the Situationist International, the associations for the vast majority of rock fans were with more familiar imagery: the Union Jack flag that Pete Townshend had worn as a jacket a decade earlier was seen again in the poster for 'Anarchy in the UK', now ripped to shreds and held together by safety-pins.

After the demise of the band, as their legacy continued to be exploited, the recently deceased Sid Vicious was to make an appearance on Virgin's advertising material, but the absence of official merchandizing of Johnny Rotten, the most photogenic star of his generation, left a gap in the market. And the high-street poster companies and the poster magazines were happy to fill that gap, disgorging lorry-loads of Rotten images that were destined to adorn bedroom walls all across suburbia, and to annoy the hell out of thousands of parents.

In the event, the decision to use Reid's artistic vision probably generated even more publicity than the fearsome sight of Rotten himself would have done. The brash, boastful sleeve to the Pistols' only proper album, *Never Mind the Bollocks, Here's the Sex Pistols* (1977), showed the title on a single-colour background with the name of the band spelt out in the now familiar blackmail lettering, and with no picture at all. Denied access to the mass media, Virgin responded by turning over their network of retail outlets to publicizing the record, with posters and displays in every window. At which stage the police moved in, threatening prosecution. In Nottingham the displays were forcibly removed and when Chris Searle, the manager of the Virgin shop there, replaced them, he found himself up in court, charged under the 1889 Indecent Advertisements Act.

This law had made it illegal to display to public view 'any picture or printed or written matter which is of an indecent or obscene nature', and the wording of Section 5 made it clear that it had been passed in response to a very specific issue in late-Victorian Britain: it covered 'any advertisement relating to syphilis, gonorrhoea, nervous debility or other complaint or infirmity arising from or relating to sexual intercourse'. At the time London was being deluged with adverts for quack remedies for sexually transmitted diseases – an increasingly common problem, or so, at least, it was believed – and respectable citizens, such as the Earl of Aberdeen, were outraged: it was impossible, he declared in the House of Lords, 'to approach the vicinity of London without seeing gateposts placarded with advertisements which come within the description contained in the Bill'. He added, in words that prefigured more than a century's worth of establishment moralizing, that it was an issue about 'corrupting the mind of youth'. As ever, it wasn't the actual existence of venereal disease to which he objected, so much as the mention of it.

There were a few dissident voices as the Bill made its way through Parliament (members who were concerned about the fate of the Venus di Milo or the works of Aristophanes under the new legislation) but there was little serious opposition, and the Act was duly passed. It was now an offence, punishable by a fine of up to forty shillings or one month in jail with hard labour, to exhibit an indecent advertisement, while the penalty for supplying such material for others to exhibit was even more severe: a fine of five pounds or up to three months' hard labour.

Within months the National Vigilance Society, a precursor of the self-appointed censors at Mary Whitehouse's Festival of Light in the 1970s, was attempting to bring cases that had little to do with the original spirit of the law (one such

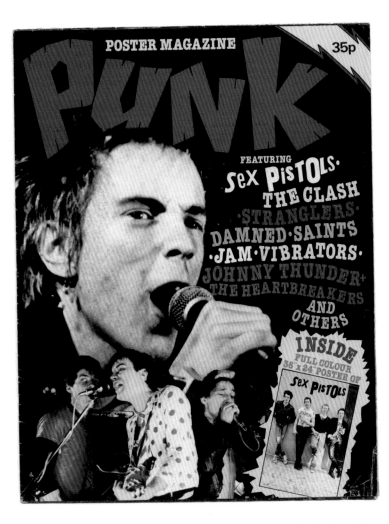

POSTER MAGAZINE

35p

PUNK

FEATURING
Sex Pistols.
THE CLASH
·STRANGLERS·
DAMNED·SAINTS
·JAM·VIBRATORS·
JOHNNY THUNDER+
THE HEARTBREAKERS
AND OTHERS

INSIDE
FULL COLOUR
36 x 24 POSTER OF
Sex Pistols

40p

PISTOL'S SCANDINAVIAN
TOUR-EXCLUSIVE PIX!

new wave
NEWS

REVOLT INTO
AUSTERITY
AND PURE
MANIA
with
Julie
Burchill

ANOTHER
ROTTEN
POSTER
INSIDE!

THE JAM...THE BOYS...THE ADVERTS....999...GENERATION X...THE HEARTBREAKERS

TOTAL PUNK!

30p

AUSTRALIA 80c   NEW ZEALAND 80c
SOUTH AFRICA 80c
MALAYSIA $2.20

GIANT
POSTER-
JOHNNY
ROTTEN
OF THE SEX PISTOLS

ALL THE
FACTS

ALL THE
PHOTO'S

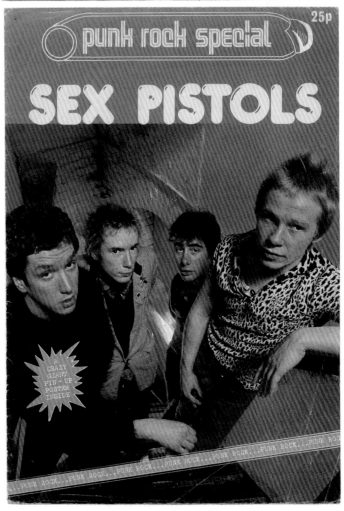

25p

punk rock special

SEX PISTOLS

A
CRAZY
GIANT
PIN-UP
POSTER
INSIDE

PUNK ROCK...PUNK ROCK...PUNK ROCK...PUNK ROCK...PUNK ROCK...PUNK ROC

concerned a depiction of a female circus performer wearing a leotard). But the very existence of the Act ensured a degree of self-censorship, and by 1907 the law had fallen into such disuse that it was being referred to in Parliament as 'a dead letter'. The foundation in 1892 of the Society for the Checking of Abuses in Public Advertising assisted the general clean-up of potentially offensive material.

Even so, the 1889 Act was still on the statute books and it was revived in 1970 to prosecute Richard Branson's charity, the Student Advisory Centre, over a leaflet that it had issued with a help-line number for those who had contracted VD; the court was unimpressed by the transparent police harassment and handed down a derisory fine of just seven pounds. Elsewhere the wider concern over the nature of rock advertising had in 1972 led to the prosecution in France of local star Michel Polnareff, whose publicity campaign included billboard posters that showed him naked, seen from behind; he was found guilty of gross indecency and fined ten francs per poster: 6,000 posters had been pasted up.

The trial of Chris Searle and Virgin Records in November 1977, therefore, was not the first time that the amoral anarchy of rock capitalism came into conflict with society's wish for ethical standards. It was, however, a much more charged affair than the industry had seen for a long time. Despite the fact that it was only tried in a magistrates court (and with the threat of hard labour having been long since lifted), it was held in the context of a full-scale media onslaught on the Pistols and punk, and it was seen as a test case by all involved: how far could these punks go with their insults to respectable society? For their defence, Virgin hired John Mortimer, QC, veteran of many of the key trials in the decensorship of Britain (including the 1971 *Oz* trial), and more recently the creator of *Rumpole of the Bailey*. Accustomed to playing on the big stage, Mortimer gave a bravura performance in front of a provincial bench of magistrates, gleefully calling witnesses to testify that the allegedly offensive word 'bollocks' had previously been used in such unimpeachable works as a medieval translation of the Bible. The verdict, delivered by Douglas Betts, chairman of the bench, was deeply grudging but nonetheless gratifying to punks everywhere: 'Much as my colleagues and I wholeheartedly deplore the vulgar exploitation of the worst instincts of human nature by both you and your company, we must reluctantly find you not guilty on each of the four charges.'

The Indecent Advertisements Act was not to survive much longer than the Pistols themselves: it was repealed in 1981 to be replaced by the Indecent Display (Control) Act, for which Mary Whitehouse had been campaigning for many years, and which was aimed primarily at the regulation of window displays by sex shops. When it was initially tabled in 1974 (this first version was lost in the snap election of February that year), the legislation was opposed by many within the rock industry, with *Melody Maker* even warning that the Sweet's stage act could fall foul of its provisions. *Plus ça change...*

LODGER

DAVID BOWIE
His new album out now on RCA

RCA

BLONDIE

ATOMIC

ATOMIC
c/w
DIE YOUNG STAY PRETTY,
HEROES'
LIMITED EDITION 7 BLACK 12 INCH SINGLE

Chrysalis

5 THE IMAGE HAS CRACKED

We were making a big impact but there was still a lot of merchandizing to be done before you could say that my property was a solid investment.
Wolf Mankowitz, *Expresso Bongo* (Ace, London, 1960)

Now, a pop group is far more like cosmetics: no one actually needs either of them. As anyone who's ever tried knows, when one is selling cosmetics packaging is everything. It's what's on the outside that counts, not what's inside, so once you've thrown away the package you've thrown away the product.
John Pidgeon, *Flame* (Panther, St Albans, 1975)

It was Doreen's room. It used to be mine and Frank's. The wallpaper had guitars and musical notes and microphones as a pattern. There were pictures of the Beatles, and the Moody Blues, and the Tremoloes and Dave Dee, Dozy, Beaky, Mick and Tich; centre-spreads from beat magazines Sellotaped on the walls. There were records and a record player in a cupboard unit next to her single bed which was made up to look like a divan, pushed against one wall.
Ted Lewis, *Jack's Return Home* (Michael Joseph, London, 1970)

On 15 November 1976, just weeks after signing their first record deal with EMI, the Sex Pistols played a gig at the Notre Dame Hall in London's Leicester Square. Amongst the audience that night were Gerry Shepherd and John Springate, the two front men from the Glitter Band, who had dressed themselves up in their finest glitter suits and platform boots for the occasion, and were still trying to make sense of the massed ranks of drainpipe jeans and short hair, when the evening's entertainment started.

'The Sex Pistols came on and did four numbers, and we left, because we'd seen enough,' remembers Springate. 'I said to Gerry: Well that's it then. I just knew. And nobody survived that. It all went bang!, fuck off, this is the new regime. Punk wiped the board with everybody.'

In truth, the Glitter Band were probably living on borrowed time by then anyway. Of the major British glam pop acts, they were the only ones who had managed a top 10 single all year; T. Rex, Slade, Sweet, Gary Glitter, Suzi Quatro, Alvin Stardust, Wizzard – all had faded away, looking pale, stale and exposed under the bright lights of disco's mirror ball. Glam had been in steep decline for nigh on eighteen months, replaced as a chart force in Britain by a new generation of teen bands, who wore matching uniforms and mined a seam of American High School pop from just before the British invasion: Mud, the Bay City Rollers, Kenny and the Rubettes. Less conceptual and more manipulated, these groups from the interregnum between glam and punk had little of the old arrogance and obsession with being stars; where Gary had insisted that he was the Leader of the Gang, the Rollers were content merely to remember the days when they 'ran with the gang'.

Above
Guillotine
A rare example of a promotional poster for a new wave compilation with artwork that was genuinely innovative and impressive. The album sleeve itself (a 10-inch record) was designed by photographer Peter Kodick, but bears no relation at all to the poster.

(Virgin Records) 29 x 19 inches, 74 x 48cm

Record companies, deciding that this was the way the wind was blowing – particularly after the Rollers confounded the critics by scoring a US #1 with 'Saturday Night' in January '76 – leapt aboard a departing bandwagon and signed up a host of groups who were intended to replicate the formula. It was not a conspicuous success. In the race to be the next teen sensations, the front runners were Bilbo Baggins, Buster, Child, Dead End Kids, Flintlock, Our Kid, Rosetta Stone, Slik and Stevenson's Rocket; between them, these acts managed just four top 10 British singles in the period 1975–78. It was a minor humiliation for the music industry, but it was a cultural disaster for the teen-magazine market that had relied on glam and white pop stars as necessary fodder for gossip and pin-ups: this corner of publishing had come to depend on pop music as its staple diet.

The role of the colour centrefold poster was not confined to the girls' magazines. *Record Mirror*, the most pop-oriented of the weekly music press, ran centrefolds through almost all of the '70s (in the late '60s they had experimented with a colour back page, ending the decade with a suitably valedictory shot of the Beatles waving goodbye), and others mimicked their lead; *Sounds* had a similar series from its launch until the economic cut-backs imposed by the three-

Top - left
New Wave
A typical piece of high-street exploitation of punk. The featured artists are (clockwise from top left) Blondie, David Bowie, Devo, the Clash, Elvis Costello, the B-52s, Graham Parker, David Byrne, Joe Jackson and Johnny Rotten.

(Europrints, Manchester, England) 24.5 x 37.5 inches 95 x 62cm

Left
Sire New Wave (1978)
The attempt to promote the bands on Sire under a single banner of new wave saw genuinely commercial prospects Talking Heads alongside less obviously mainstream acts, including the Dead Boys and Voidoids, from the New York scene, and the Saints, from Australia. Ken Kushnick of Sire was later to comment: 'We spent a campaign's worth of time, money, and effort on those four records, and only one walked away from the rest – the Heads.'

(Sire) 23 x 35 inches, 89 x 58cm

Right
Buzzcocks - 'Orgasm Addict'
The first single by Buzzcocks on a major label, 'Orgasm Addict' was released in October 1977. Its sleeve, based on a collage by Linder Sterling, introduced a vein of aggressive surrealism to punk that pointed a way forward away from the glam tradition. The design was by Malcolm Garrett and the lettering and lines were executed on a drawing board, as can be seen at full poster size in the ink bleeds at the start of the lines.

Design Malcolm Garrett, artwork Linder Sterling (United Artists) 29 x 38.5 inches, 98 x 73.5cm

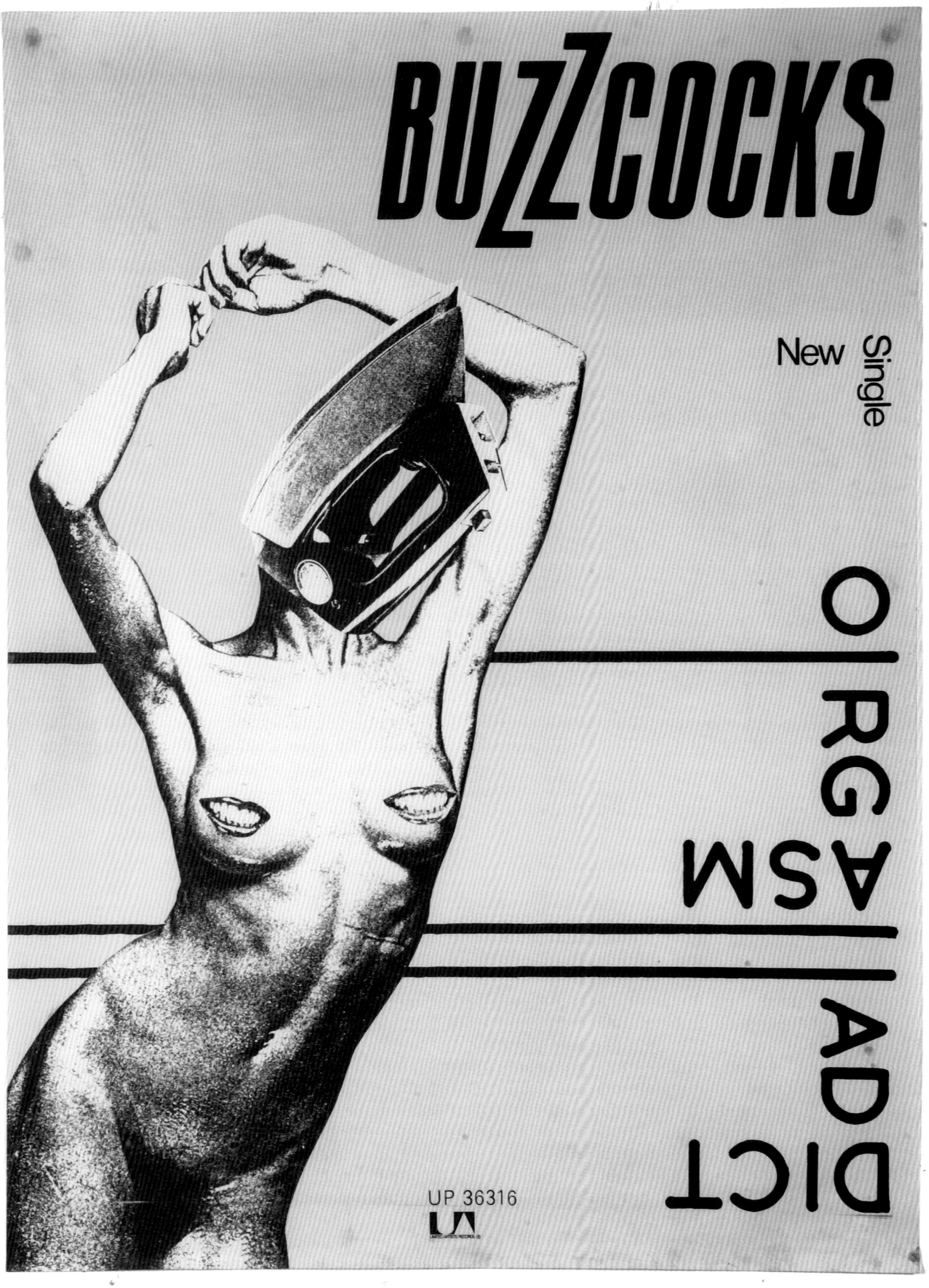

BUZZCOCKS

New Single

ORGASM ADDICT

UP 36316

day week of 1974, and *Disc* too featured a pull-out-and-stick-up poster before it was swallowed up by *Record Mirror* in '75. The intention was two-fold: to offer the readers a cheap poster of their idols, and to achieve the domestic advertising that Alice Cooper had exploited with the 1972 calendar; an image of a glammed-up Eno bearing the logo of *Disc* was a sound piece of symbiotic marketing that was in everyone's interests. (Though the confused nature of the times could be seen in a double-page colour poster advert in *Disc* for *Diamond Dogs* that had a pin-up of the Rollers on the other side.)

It was, however, the straight teen magazines – the likes of *Jackie*, *Diana*, *Look-In* and *Fab 208* – that specialized in such pin-ups. *Jackie*, as the market leader, was particularly adventurous, on one occasion commissioning an original painting of Marc Bolan by George Underwood for inclusion, and on another serializing a Keith Morris photo of Bolan over a three-week period: to ensure that one kept buying, it started with the feet and legs and finally the face, building into a full-scale poster for Marc fans. The practice was not entirely new: Peter Blake's piece 'Knife Thrower's Board' (1957) had been based on a life-size picture of Brigitte Bardot that had been issued in weekly parts by *Reveille*. And in 1977 Stiff Records took the concept a stage further by releasing a part-work poster of Elvis Costello to promote his debut album, *My Aim Is True*; the novelty here was that the separate sections were issued in a single week as double-page adverts in the three leading music papers, *NME*, *Sounds* and *Melody Maker*.

Above
Stiff Records (1976)
A poster celebrating the first eight singles released on Stiff, and illustrating the range of artists on the label.

Design Chris Morton (Stiff) 20 x 30 inches, 76 x 50.5cm

Left
Elvis Costello – *My Aim Is True* (1977)
The cover of Costello's debut album emphasized his image as, in the words of manager and label-owner Jake Riviera, 'Buddy Holly on acid'. The poster dispensed with the chequerboard background of the original to focus exclusively on the photo.

Photography Keith Morris (Stiff Records) 20 x 30 inches, 77.5 x 51cm

Springate's analysis of the impact of punk was absolutely correct. The arrival of the Pistols sent waves of horror crashing though the chart world. When various pop stars were asked by *Record Mirror* in December '76 what had been the worst thing about the year, there was near consensus: 'Punk rock,' said Les Grey of Mud; 'there must have been such an awful lot of talent going to waste because every record company just wanted to book such lousy bands.' Hugh McDowell of ELO managed to combine the death of Benjamin Britten and punk as a double nomination, while Britain's first disco queen, Tina Charles, went for the seismically insecure moral high ground: 'The worst thing was punk rock; I'm patriotic and I didn't like the way they were being nasty about the Queen.'

The teen magazines tried to weather the storm by concentrating on TV stars like Starsky & Hutch and Henry Winkler's incarnation as the Fonz in *Happy Days*, but the reliance on pop remained and the need for new flesh to stoke up the fires of fandom was insatiable. And if glam was dead, and disco was too black for pin-ups, then maybe the answer was punk; after all, Midge Ure of Slik had been Malcolm McLaren's first choice as singer with the Sex Pistols, Billy Idol looked like a star, even though the public seemed to prefer Billy Ocean, and Eater were young if not very pretty. In desperation, the teen industry attempted to co-opt the better looking punks into the agenda, and so it was that, for example, Eddie & the Hot Rods made an appearance as a centrefold pin-up in *Blue Jeans* in 1977. (Their singer Barrie Masters had more than his fair share of such moments: 'I was even a Page 7 Fella in the *Sun*,' he remembers. 'I cringe with embarrassment.') Less apologetic was Ian Pain of New Hearts, later to become Ian Page of Secret Affair: 'So many of the bands consider it to be so unhip to be in *Pink*,' he said in 1978. 'But you'd be surprised at the amount of teenage punk girls that buy *Mates* and all those magazines.'

For those concerned with their credibility, though, it was a worrying development. 'There'd be big centre-page things in *Record Mirror* and we were on the cover of *Smash Hits* once,' recalls Poly Styrene. 'That's when I told my manager: I don't want to do this any more. It was the way it was marketed; I thought it was overly commercial.'

134

Below

CBGBs – 10th anniversary
In 1974 Max's Kansas City wasn't staging gigs, the Mercer Arts Center had (literally) collapsed and the New York live circuit needed a new outlet. Tom Verlaine and Richard Hell identified the solution with a Hell's Angels hangout in the Bowery known as CBGBs. 'Needing our own niche,' wrote Patti Smith, 'they found an untapped derelict bar on the Bowery. The proprietor, Hilly Crystal, allowed a small stage to be built and CBGBs became ours.' It was soon known as the home of the emergent punk scene, and is still celebrated as the rock club most closely associated with the city.

(CBGBs) 23 x 35 inches, 89 x 58.5cm

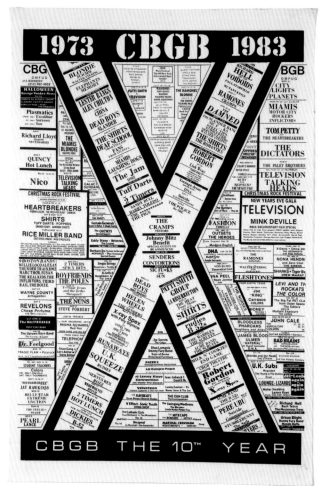

Opposite

A Nite At Max's Kansas City (1985)
Max's Kansas City opened in 1965 at 213 Park Avenue South between 17th and 18th, off Union Square, New York. Initially a haunt of the art scene, it became increasingly associated with rock & roll after the Velvet Underground's performances there. 'Max's was the place where all the different scenes crossed and merged,' wrote Jayne County, 'the gay scene, the drug scene, the theatre scene, the music scene, the art scene.'

Amongst those who worked at Max's were Wayne County as DJ and Debbie Harry as a waitress, whilst Bob Marley, Bruce Springsteen and Madonna played early gigs upstairs. It closed in 1982, but the continuing potency of its name is apparent from this poster.

23 x 35 inches, 89 x 58.5cm

This attempt to subsume punk into the mainstream of pop was always doomed to failure – no self-respecting teenybopper wanted anything to do with these spotty yobbos who seemed more interested in substance abuse than in personal hygiene – but the market had more than one way of neutering a cat.

In America the dominant response was to ignore the entire phenomenon. The attitude towards punk by most in the record business was to turn away, hum a Supertramp song to themselves and hope that the whole thing disappeared. The US establishment was so fearsomely conservative when it came to rock & roll that as late as 1981 the magazine *Record World* could still name the Moody Blues as Most Promising Male Band; two years later the Beach Boys were banned from appearing at the official Fourth of July celebrations in Washington because the Secretary of the Interior feared they would 'attract an undesirable element'. With the nation suffering a social and political crisis of faith, this was no time to rock the boat: a moral panic about degenerate music was the last thing the business needed. Besides, there were perfectly respectable profits to be made elsewhere.

The leading New York bands did secure recording contracts, but the companies involved (Sire, Private Stock, Red Star) were far from being the most high-profile, and their promotional budgets simply couldn't match those of the really big players; consequently the music was seldom heard on the all-powerful radio stations. When the Sex Pistols, as the most heavily touted British punks, arrived in the States in 1978 for a chaotic and disastrous tour that ended in the band splitting up, and when Sid Vicious died of a heroin overdose a year later in New York, whilst on bail charged with murder, the music industry indulged in a delightful shudder at this confirmation of its prejudices. It had always known that punk was nasty and self-destructive, and the negative fallout from the Pistols' tour ensured that the status quo remained. Blondie and Talking Heads successfully escaped the taint by making their music more radio-friendly, but the more hardcore bands – the Heartbreakers, the Voidoids – were left behind; the Ramones, in a twenty-year recording career, failed to reach the top 40 albums chart in the US.

Knowing that it had to compete with hostility towards not only the music but New York itself, Sire Records attempted to cushion the blow and launched a promotional campaign in 1977 under the slogan: 'New wave rock & roll, Get behind it before it gets past you'. The phrase 'new wave' (reputedly coined by Sire boss, Seymour Stein, from the '50s French cinema movement, *la nouvelle vague*) was to become a soft synonym for punk, and was subsequently used to describe almost any band that signed a record deal in 1977–79.

Other advertising campaigns of the time sought to ally existing artists to punk, a two-way process that chased credibility by association but also helped reduce the shock of the new; the two New York Dolls records were reissued as a double album under the slogan, 'Before anyone discovered New Wave Rock, the Dolls were inventing it'. Elsewhere Arista was pushing Lou Reed, the Kinks and Patti Smith as 'the originators' and suggesting that we shouldn't concern ourselves overmuch with 'the imitators'; and even the Beatles saw a tape of themselves performing at the Star Club, Hamburg finally released in 1977, and sold as being from a time 'when your Granny wouldn't have liked them'.

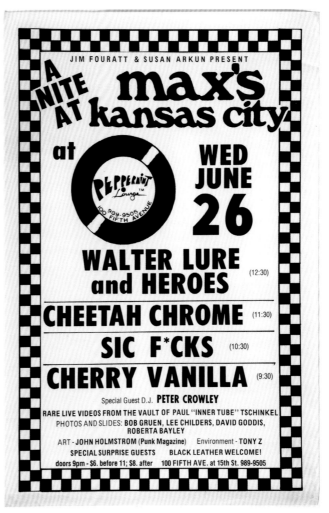

135

POWER IN THE DARKNESS

TOM ROBINSON BAND

ON HARVEST RECORDS AND TAPES   AVAILABLE FROM CAPITOL RECORDS

(Soon afterwards the notorious 'butcher cover' of their 1966 album *Yesterday and Today* appeared on an unofficial poster in London, showing the sleeve nestling amidst even more meat and doll parts than were on the original photo; Alice himself would have hesitated over such tasteless imagery.)

None of this could quite match the crass cynicism of the earlier promotion of rock on CBS, which in 1971 finally abandoned its absurd slogan 'The man can't bust our music', to replace it with the marginally less embarrassing 'The revolutionaries are on Columbia'. Equally, however, none of them reached the heights of Stiff Records which, under the direction of former advertising man Jake Riviera, produced a series of instantly memorable slogans on an almost weekly basis, reaching a peak of sorts with the cheerfully obscene: 'If it ain't a Stiff, it ain't worth a fuck'.

But then the intentions were very different. Stiff was in the business of building a cult brand, trumpeting their independent quirkiness to a minority market, while Sire wanted to shift its bands into the mainstream. Neither excuse could be called upon to justify the Europrints 'New Wave' poster; it merely rounded up a few loose artists, including Bowie, Graham Parker and Joe Jackson (the latter getting a picture six times larger than that of Johnny Rotten), and hoped to make a few quid out of the least hip people in Britain.

'Punk is at the moment undergoing a fate worse than death in that it is starting to be catered for,' wrote Danny Baker, more in anger than sorrow, in the August 1977 edition of *ZigZag* magazine. He was talking about the Vortex, the mostly unloved London club that followed on from the revered Roxy, but it was a wider truth about how the scene was already being corralled, under the name of new wave, back into the flock.

Within a couple of years, punk had acquired a nostalgia value. British punks – now with neat Mohican haircuts and sporting a form of traditional dress that was as impressive and as convincing as a member of the royal family in a kilt – were part of the tourist map of London, charging for snapshots and being sold on postcards. From a position of wanting to change everything, or at the very least rock & roll, punk had instead quietly taken its place in the carnival procession of youth cults.

Tom Robinson Band – *Power in the Darkness* (1978)
'I think it was Syd Shelton or Roger Huddle from Rock Against Racism who put the logo together for me,' remembers Tom Robinson. 'I specified I wanted the lettering in a stencil typeface around a fist in bright yellow on a black background. They found the fist on a miners's trade union poster of the early twentieth century, nicked the design and assembled the logo accordingly. (I'd nicked the basic idea of lettering around a fist myself - from the early 1970s UK Gay Liberation Front badge.) We had the logo long before we had a record deal: taking our cue from the Sex Pistols, the band's visual identity in terms of graphics was a key part of what we did.'
The stencilled fist was later used by the Socialist Workers Party, who had been the principal political backers of Rock Against Racism

Photography Terry O'Neill (Harvest Records) 20 x 30 inches, 76 x 50.5cm

The Clash – *Black Market Clash* (1980)
The poster for this US compilation of Clash singles and b-sides was based on a photograph of film-maker Don Letts facing a line of police at the start of the rioting at the 1976 Notting Hill Carnival. 'That picture looks like I am walking towards the cops,' Letts recalled. 'I am actually walking across the road. Behind me there are about 5,000 brothers all bricked up ready to throw.'
The collage addition of the military hardware, as well as the trimming of the photo (the line of police is longer in the original) detracts from the power of the image, but the intention of establishing the band at the heart of urban confrontation is clear: this is the London that the band and/or record label wanted to portray to America. As the Secretary of State for Energy, Tony Benn, once pointed out: 'The Clash are apparently very popular with working-class youngsters who don't find anything in our popular culture that meets their needs or reflects their feelings.'

(Epic) 30 x 48 inches, 89 x 58cm

The Clash – *London Calling* (1979)
Like the Rolling Stones, the Clash seldom appeared on their official posters, but this is an exception. Based on Ray Lowry's sleeve design for the third album, with its conscious echo of Elvis Presley's debut album, this was aimed at record shops, with the emphasis on the bargain price of the double album: 'Two For A Fiver!'

Photography Pennie Smith; design Ray Lowry (CBS) 24 x 24 inches, 61 x 61cm

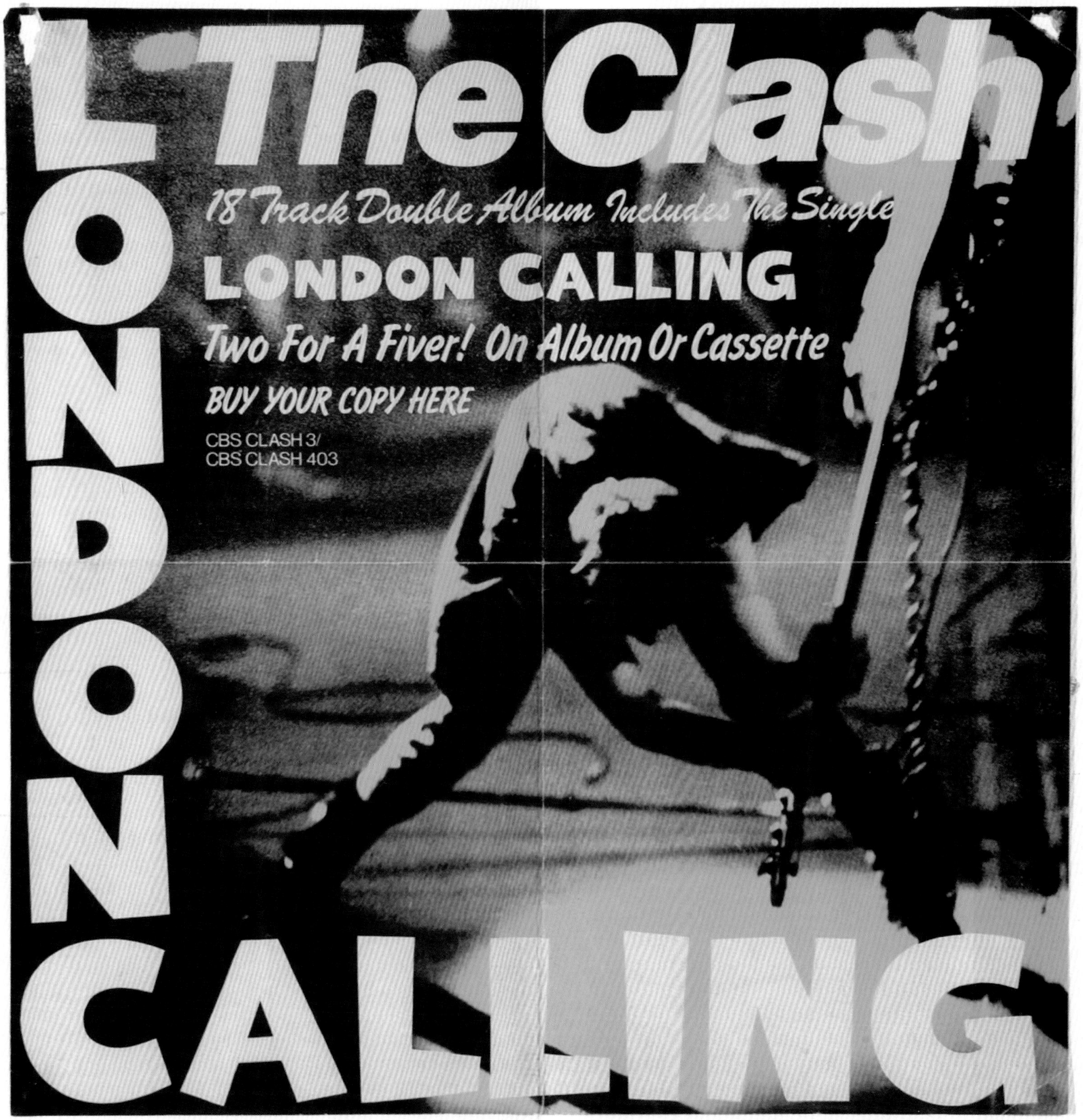
The Clash
18 Track Double Album Includes The Single
LONDON CALLING
Two For A Fiver! On Album Or Cassette
BUY YOUR COPY HERE
CBS CLASH 3/
CBS CLASH 403
LONDON
CALLING

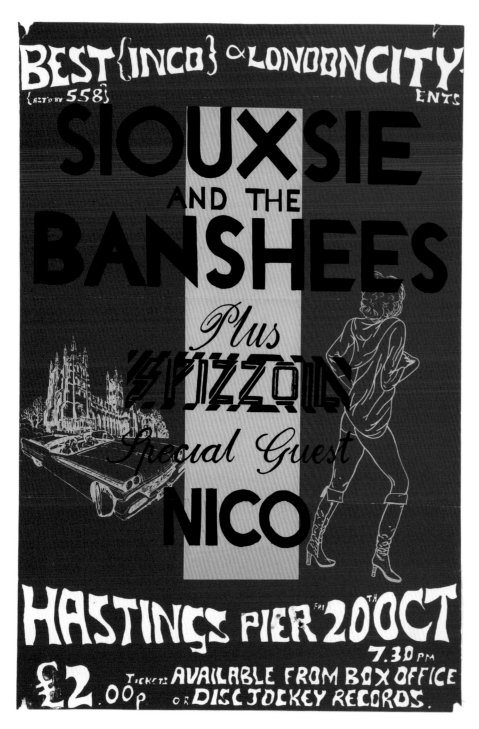

By 1978 it was clear that a moment had passed. *Sniffin' Glue* closed in February, Television split in August, and in October Nancy Spungeon was murdered, possibly by Sid Vicious. Meanwhile Patti Smith was enjoying chart success in Britain with 'Because the Night', a song co-written by Bruce Springsteen, and debut hits for Devo, Siouxsie & the Banshees and John Lydon's new band Public Image Ltd suggested that the more creative end of punk had lost patience with the formal limitations of the music and the dirigiste attitude of the London elite. 'Punk started out with the idea of being original,' says Poly Styrene, 'but then later you had to conform to the punk mould.'

The death of punk in Britain mirrored the death of glam, which had in turn mirrored that of mod. Again, punk had been at its best a combination of working-class youth and art-school sensibilities, and again, the coalition had fallen apart when the artistic wing made its excuses and left, seeking new forms and fresh challenges. The key difference was that punk had failed to make a serious commercial impact. In fact it looked almost as though British rock was in the grip of a law of diminishing returns. The mid-'60s bands had impacted right across the western world; then glam had swept Britain and much of Europe, but been

Above

Siouxsie & the Banshees – Live (1978)
A curious poster for a curious end-of-the-pier show. The illustrations give no indication at all of the nature of the bands involved.

Right

Public Image Ltd – Live (1980)
More than two years after leaving the Sex Pistols and reverting to his real name, John Lydon was still being billed in Los Angeles as 'formerly Johnny Rotten of the Sex Pistols'. Support act Los Plugz were a Latino punk band, and at their suggestion a new band named Los Lobos were added to the bottom of the bill.

17 x 22 inches, 55.5 x 43cm

PRESENTS

PUBLIC IMAGE

JOHN LYDON   KEITH LEVENE   WOBBLE

formerly Johnny Rotten
of the *Sex Pistols*

LOS PLUGZ
and THE
KIPPER KIDS
+ SPECIAL
GUESTS

SUNDAY 8 PM
MAY 4

GENERAL ADMISSION
$8.50 ADVANCE
$10.00 AT THE DOOR

OLYMPIC
AUDITORIUM
TICKETS: BOX OFFICE RI9-5171
TICKETRON 642-5700

unable to make a major breakthrough in America. Now punk struggled even to get a handful of hit singles at home (with the very special exception of the Sex Pistols), and did absolutely nothing in an American chart that was dominated in 1977 by the ten-week reign at #1 of Pat Boone's daughter, Debby, singing 'You Light Up My Life'. And although new wave bands had more success, they too paled in comparison with the all-conquering power of disco, even when they came up with a revered pop classic like the Undertones' first single 'Teenage Kicks', a record which couldn't crack the top 30 when released in 1978.

Something had changed since the '60s, and arguably what was different was society itself.

Initially at least, the class coalition in British rock reflected a wider social perspective, in which postwar Britain was itself the product of a coalition between a left-leaning intelligentsia and the trade unions. The alliance of forces reached a peak in the early '60s, when it became clear that Harold Wilson's Labour Party was about to return to power, and when swinging Britain began to sell the myth of classlessness both to itself and to the world beyond.

In reality this putative democracy was little more than a slightly confused stab at meritocracy (a word that had rapidly dropped the pejorative connotations intended by Michael Young when he invented it in 1958), and was a subject for mockery from the outset; in the 1961 *Beyond the Fringe* sketch 'Real Class', Peter Cook nonchalantly drawled that 'Jonathan Miller and myself come from good families and have had the benefits of a public-school education,' whereas the other half of the team (Alan Bennett and Dudley Moore) had 'worked their way up from working-class origins'. But despite the parodies, classlessness was a persuasive tale, and popular culture delighted in its telling. For the first time it became not just fashionable but commonplace for accents to be downwardly mobile, for footballers to be mentioned alongside civil servants in the Queen's Birthday Honours List, and for the absence of privilege to be celebrated.

In rock & roll the influence of the public-school element tended to come from outside the groups, from management and from characters such as Robert Fraser, rather than from within (with the very occasional exception of a band like Genesis: rarer than hens' teeth and much less interesting).

But to maintain the image of the classless society, it was important that the establishment should be seen as embracing and endorsing a token few from outside its ranks, as *The Times* demonstrated in its famous 1967 editorial in support of Mick Jagger, after he was sentenced to gaol for possession of drugs ('Who breaks a butterfly on a wheel?'). Again there were diminishing returns: Bowie was accepted but to a lesser degree than Jagger, whilst Johnny Rotten was very definitely seen as being a step too far.

The problem was that by the early '70s the cultural side of consensus politics was starting to fragment, resulting in moral panics about rampant trade unionism and about working-class youth culture (primarily skinheads and football hooligans), and by the time of punk the economic element of that consensus had collapsed completely: three decades of Keynesian policy was being swept away by the advent of monetarism.

In an increasingly fractured society, the culture of pop also disintegrated: dancing on a Saturday night still provided the public escape from the tedium of work, and the private retreat into artistic self-expression was still catered for, but punk, which had sought, like mod and glam before it, to marry the two spheres, failed to do so. Social collapse did not preclude creativity, as New York had already demonstrated (certainly to the satisfaction of *Rolling Stone*, which moved its head office there from San Francisco in 1977), but it did make it harder to find a mass market for art rock.

(Parenthetically, it might be noted that in due course a new social coalition was built when right-wing intellectuals combined with disaffected working-class voters to usher in Thatcherism. It wasn't, perhaps, entirely an accident that the highpoint of Margaret Thatcher's popularity – the landslide 1983 election in the wake of the Falklands War – also saw the second British invasion of the US charts.)

Right

XTC – *White Music* (1978)
Photographer Dennis Morris got his big break at the age of fourteen when Bob Marley found him waiting to catch a Wailers soundcheck at the Speakeasy Club in London, and invited him to join the band on tour. When the Sex Pistols signed to Virgin Records, Johnny Rotten asked that he take the first official photos of the group. The picture on the sleeve of XTC's debut album is less celebrated but was an influential statement of how new wave, as opposed to punk, bands were to present themselves in the UK.

Photography Dennis Morris; design & photographic effects Cooke Key (Virgin) 19 x 28 inches, 71 x 48cm

There were, of course, those who survived the demise of punk. Most of those who did so – the Jam, the Clash, Elvis Costello – took their inspiration from the more folk-based traditions within pop: soul, r&b, country, reggae and rockabilly. Their music was filtered through a mod-glam-punk attitude, but it was essentially backward looking, reasserting the value of roots and authenticity. The one key exception was Adam Ant, who prefigured much of what was to come.

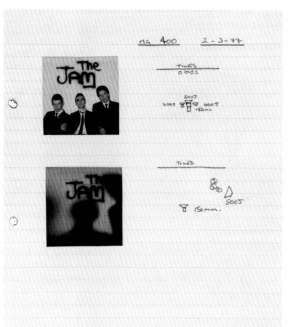

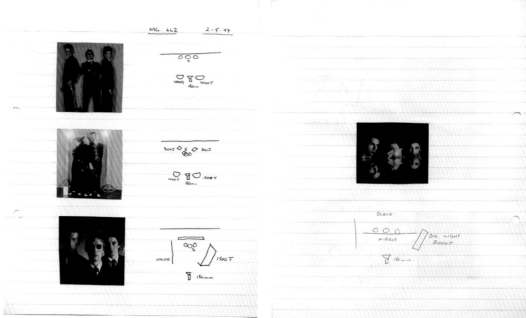

In his student days as Stuart Goddard, Adam had been a member of the North London art band Bazooka Joe (whose act included staged fights, complete with mock blood, a routine borrowed from Vince Taylor). It was at one of their gigs, at St Martin's College of Art in November 1975, that the Sex Pistols made their public debut; suitably impressed by the support act, Goddard began the wild mutation into a rock & roll star. Through the punk era Adam & the Ants, in an ever-changing line-up, occupied a position that was somehow both prominent and yet peripheral. They attracted a substantial cult following, but their celebration of sex – at a time when rock & roll was curiously unerotic – and their clear debt to the glam tradition made them unpopular with the 'excitable personalities' in the music press, and they were never accorded a place in the critical pantheon. Nor did they come close to touching a broader audience, due, in no small measure, to Adam's image: the barely suppressed violence of his stage persona and the fetish-driven monochrome montages he produced as artwork were almost calculated to alienate the major record companies.

In January 1980 the entire sixth incarnation of the Ants split from him (going on to become Bow Wow Wow under Malcolm McLaren's management) and, forced into a rethink, Adam found a guitarist and songwriting partner in Marco Perroni, a Mick Ronson figure to assist his rise to stardom. With a two-drummer line-up

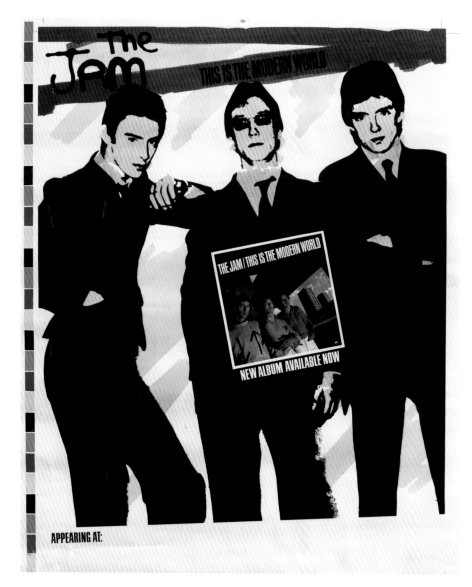

Left

The Jam – *This is the Modern World* (1977)
A combination of the photo used on the sleeve of
the single 'The Modern World' with (inset) the
album of the same name. This is a proof copy, as
seen in the colour guide on the left margin.

Main photograph Martyn Goddard; album
photography Gerard Mankowitz; design Bill Smith
(Polydor)

inspired by the Glitter Band, and with a CBS recording contract in the pocket of
their black leather trousers, the new version of the Ants replicated Marc Bolan's
belated overnight success; by the end of '81 they'd achieved seven top 10 singles
and three hit albums and were the biggest pop group in the country.

The music was now a patchwork of tribal drums, twangy guitar and heroic
backing vocals, while the lyrics ranged freely over native Americans, pirates,
highwaymen, fairy tales and anything else Adam could conjure up from the
repository of shared cultural memories, all placed within the most unashamed
self-celebration heard since Mott The Hoople. It was pop art masquerading as
pop music, and Adam was completely conscious of his intention to become a
star: 'I made the decision to focus on me. Whereas the *Dirk Wears White Sox*
cover was very esoteric and mysterious, *Kings of the Wild Frontier* was right in
your face. And it worked, and once we went on TV, that was the way to go.' So
did he see himself as continuing the tradition of Bolan, Roxy Music and Lou
Reed? 'Absolutely, 100%. Because they were doing the best work on the planet,
they were the kings of glam.'

Right

The Only Ones – Planet Tour (1978)
One of the most perplexing (and biggest) posters
of the new wave era, this silkscreen masterpiece
features a '50s sci-fi typeface that the band never
used in any other context, a dinosaur that has no
known connection with the music and a strong
but unglamorous poker hand. What any of it
means is anyone's guess, but it's a striking – if
arbitrary – collection of images.

Design Kavanagh, 30.5 x 41 inches; 104 x 77cm

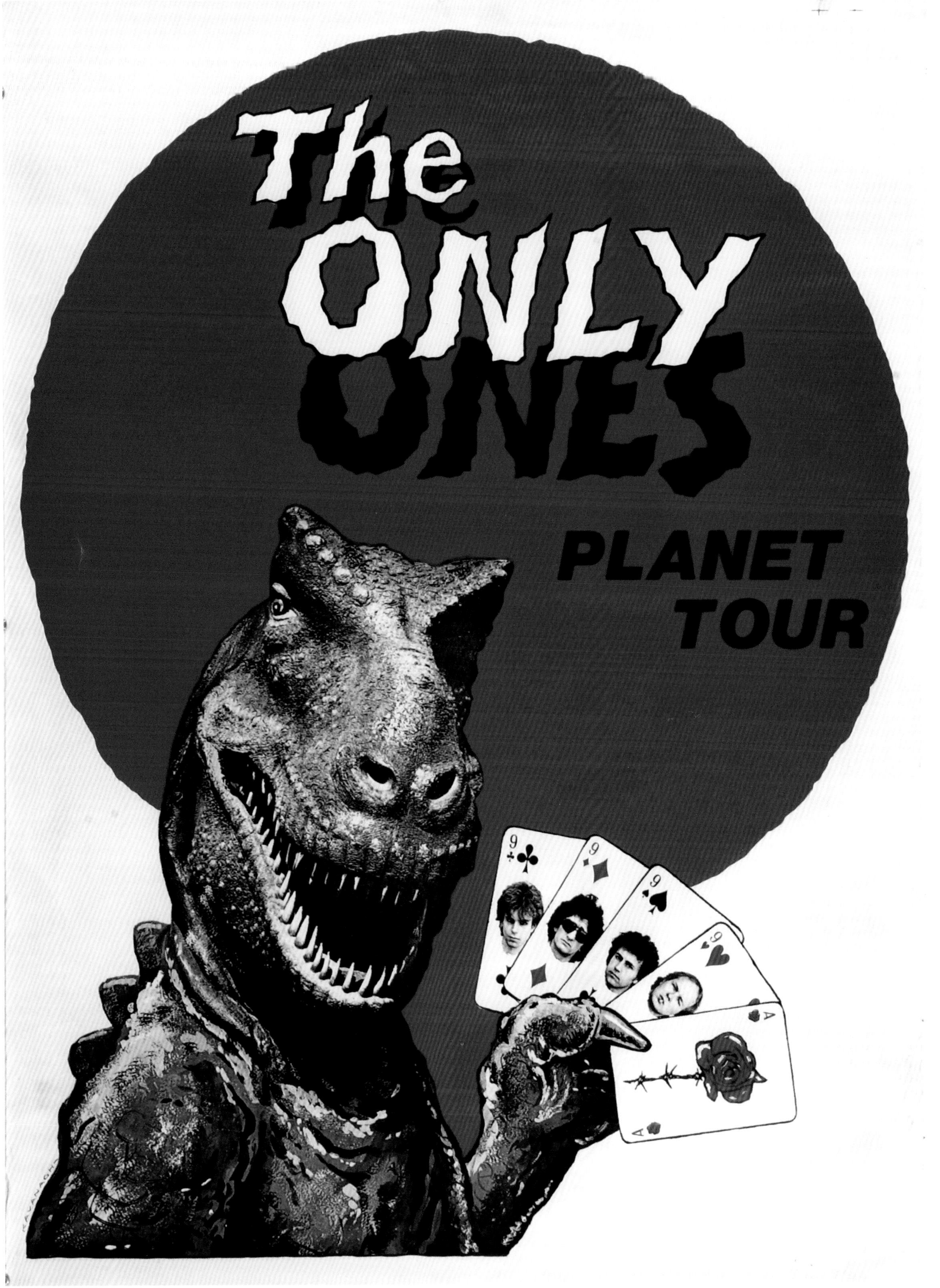
The ONLY ONES
PLANET TOUR

ADAM&THE

KINGS OF THE WILD FRONTIER

the new single

ANTS

The Ants were the last of the great glam bands, but also the first of a new age of media-friendly acts who knew the power of marketing. 'I think merchandising came in with our era, because we were pop fans,' Marco argues. 'Some bands thought: we can't do all the merchandising because it looks a little bit naff, or capitalistic. But we thought: we'll do everything we can possibly think of. Because that's what we liked. We wanted to be a pop band, and we wanted to recreate our youths as glam fans.'

A generation that had grown up with posters of Bolan and Alice Cooper on their bedroom walls was supremely aware of the power of imagery. David Essex's self-deprecatingly cynical 1974 hit 'Gonna Make You A Star' had mocked the malleability of musicians: 'He says he's into his music, but I don't believe it; he just doesn't seem to understand the rock media,' but no such charge could be laid at Adam's door; he even went to court to argue that his make-up constituted a work of art and was therefore his copyright property. (The judge disagreed and ruled that the temporary nature of cosmetics precluded any such claim.)

Despite that setback, the Ants embraced pop in a way that no other British post-punk band yet had: they revelled in *Top of the Pops* (a programme on which their label mates, the Clash, refused ever to appear), they spoke to the glossy pop magazine *Smash Hits* rather than the *NME*, and they took with enthusiasm to the new medium of video – the photos on the cover of the *Wild Frontier* album were stills from their self-financed promo for the first single. They also licensed firms to make posters of them.

This development of the official, licensed poster was comparatively recent. When mass-produced posters first began to appear in the high street, they seldom brought any remuneration to the acts featured on them. 'Most of the posters that were put out were done by outside companies and we didn't even know about them all the time,' reflects Alice Cooper. 'Who knows if we ever got paid for them? We had more control over our promotional posters and not the ones that were sold in stores.'

By the mid-'70s the more astute of the commercial companies were signing up stars on exclusive deals. Most successful at the time was probably the Ohio-based Pro Arts Inc, run by Ted Trikilis, who began with images of Bruce Lee and Elton John and the like, and made it really big when he licensed a photograph of Farrah Fawcett a few months before the TV series *Charlie's Angels* was screened in 1976; two years later he was claiming that the picture had been reproduced more than a hundred million times, not just on posters but also on T-shirts, badges and other merchandizing. (Britain's most famous poster of the period was Martin Elliott's photograph 'Tennis Girl', which was launched in '77 and sold upwards of two million copies.) It was a new initiative in mass-merchandizing, and over the next decade poster firms followed the model of music publishers and began acting as talent scouts, offering cash advances to promising new bands in exchange for rights that might become worth big money.

Previous page and right
Adam & the Ants – *Kings of the Wild Frontier* (1980)
The break between the old Ants style (p.115) and his rebirth as a pop star was entirely deliberate. 'When I did *Kings of the Wild Frontier* I just wanted it ultra-colourful,' he says. 'I'd had four years of doing black-and-white and now I had access to doing colour and it was great. It was much more focused on me.' The title track was released as a single four months before the album but made little impact – it was only when the full-colour incarnation was unveiled that Antmania really took off.

Previous page
Photography Barbara; design Adam Ant (CBS Records) 30 x 40 inches, 101.5 x 76cm
Right
Design Adam Ant (CBS Records) 24 x 36 inches, 91.5 x 61cm

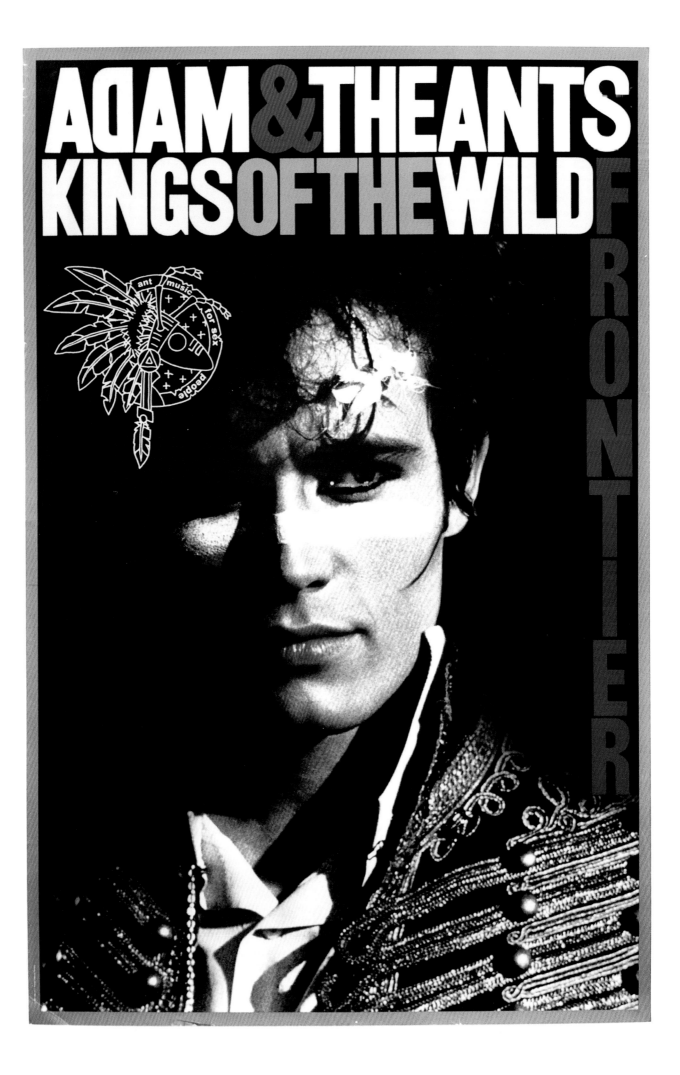

Left

The Adverts - *Crossing the Red Sea with the Adverts* (1978)
One of the classic records to come out of British punk, the first Adverts album featured a sleeve designed by Nicholas De Ville, who was better known for his work with Roxy Music but who had also created the sleeve for the Adverts' single 'Gary Gilmore's Eyes'. The poster, however, was a three-colour screen print based on a photocopy of a different image.

152

27.5 x 40 inches, 101.5 x 70cm

'CROSSING THE RED SEA'

WITH THE

'ERTS

FIRST ALBUM

IGGY POP

Special Guests:
The Human League

Tourneeleitung:
Karsten Jahnke
Konzertdirektion
Hamburg 13

Neue LP
Iggy Pop
NEW VALUES
1 C-064-62699
ARISTA Record & Tapes
Vertrieb in Deutschland:
EMI Electrola GmbH

Iggy Pop - live (1979)
**Iggy's European tour to promote his *New Values*
album saw him supported by the Human League,
who had just signed to Virgin after two
independent singles and were already being
touted by David Bowie as 'the future of pop
music.'**

Above

***ZigZag* magazine**
**A page from issue #90 (December 1978)
advertising a special offer on Debbie Harry
posters.**

The value of authorized merchandise had been identified in the pre-Beatles era, as Royston Ellis spelt out in his 1964 novel of the era, *Myself For Fame*: 'So many stars lose a mint of loot because they don't think about this. Every theatre you play when you're on tour, you'll find that there are men outside selling photographs of you at 2/6 a time. That's nearly 2/6 profit to them you know. If you make sure that only authorized pictures of you are on sale, and charge a royalty for that authorization, you'll do okay.' Actually enforcing such a decision in relation to posters proved more of a challenge: 'When we used to tour, we had all these sellers of posters and merchandise that followed us,' remembers the Bay City Rollers' manager, Tam Paton. 'We never made any money out of those at all. They made up pictures, copied pictures out of magazines. We sold the posters inside, but we couldn't harm the people selling this pirate stuff outside.' Adam Ant's response to the same phenomenon five years later was equally irritated, but he saw it also as a challenge: 'Your merchandizing has to be really fucking good so the fans will go for the real deal. Especially when you're dealing with young kids, 'cos they'll get so excited they'll buy anything.'

Paton adopted a total marketing approach to the Rollers. 'I was selling an image,' he says. 'I had to control it because I was aware that all I had was an image.' When the band did a photo session for a magazine, he insisted on choosing the shot that would be used and destroying all the out-takes: 'I never looked at a picture without the negative being there. And we used to destroy loads and loads of negatives. I used to cut them up physically myself with scissors.' He applied the same attention to detail elsewhere: 'I used to keep in control of the fan club at the same time. We used to ask who their favourite Roller was, and when I found any member of the Rollers was falling behind big-style, I would then concentrate on them, getting them press, photographing them, trying to push them ahead.'

Within a couple of years, fan clubs too had become big business. Adam Ant was one of the few punks to appreciate their potential value in building band and brand loyalty: 'The packs we sent out had six black-and-white photographs, a set of badges and one of the handbills. They'd send an S.A.E. and that was it. And there were probably over a thousand members in 1978 from all over the country.' But this was the home-industry version. In America Pro Arts Inc had expanded from posters into running professional clubs for suitably safe stars such as Olivia Newton-John and Shaun Cassidy; for a five-dollar subscription, the fan received photos, postcards and 'a poster that is not available in any retail store anywhere in the country'.

The move to an increasingly professional approach to marketing can be seen in a series of snapshots. In 1978 *ZigZag* magazine in the UK was offering readers a special deal on two Debbie Harry posters at one pound each (inc. p&p); two years later she was a big enough household name that Smith's Crisps were giving away a poster of her in exchange for proofs of purchase. This was still within the same scope as the *Sun*'s Bolan poster in 1972, but in the new decade sponsorship really kicked in: on the 1982 Roxy Music tour every audience member was issued with a poster of the band advertising Levi's new range of

Left

Motörhead – England (1977)
Designed by Joe Petagno in 1975, the logo for Lemmy's post-Hawkwind band Motörhead has proved one of the most enduring and potent images in British rock. The original design featured a skull based on a cross between a gorilla, a wolf and a dog, with boar's tusks, to which Lemmy added the accessories – helmet, chains, military insignia. Petagno: 'It was meant to be read as a biker symbol, a call to arms, so to speak.'

Design Joe Petagno

Right

Johnny Thunders – Live (1982)
The support act for this Johnny Thunders gig was Bebe Buell, former member of the GTOs, whose relationships with musicians ('I've lived my life as somewhat of a muse,' she once said) included Steve Tyler of Aerosmith, a union that produced Liv Tyler.

Photography Marcia Resnick; design Steve Keister; 25 x 38 inches, 96.5 x 63.5cm

black jeans. It was a terrifying intimation of commercial tie-ins to come; the band that had defined cool ten years earlier were now flogging mass-market denim (though Ferry took care to dress in white trousers for the photo); for Levi's the cool-by-association image gain was clear; for Roxy the benefit was purely pecuniary.

But perhaps such rewards were long overdue. That 1978 *ZigZag* special offer came with a plaintive quote from Debbie Harry: 'There are all these posters out, and there's only one of them I get the money from.'

FRANZ-CHRISTOPH GIERCKE/HALFWAY HOUSE PRODUCTIONS PRESENTS:

LAST CONCERT   EUROPEAN TOUR

BEFORE

BYE - BYE

PHOTO: MARCIA RESNICK

JOHNNY THUNDERS

DESIGN: STEVE KEISTER ©1982

SATURDAY MARCH 13   W/ BEBE BUELL

IRVING PLAZA   17 IRVING PLACE   533-9427

DOORS OPEN 10 PM   ADVANCE TICKETS $7.50

FREE BEING RECORDS   ROCKS IN YOUR HEAD

SWEET "B"   FIORRUCCI

BLEEKER BOB'S

THE CRAMPS

gs The Lord Taught Us
The Album

EDIE
Ciao!
MANHATTAN
THE WRECK OF A WARHOL SUPERSTAR

DEBORAH HARRY
BLON

CHANGESONEBOWIE

HIS GREATEST HITS.
"Space Oddity," "Changes," "Ziggy Stardust," "Suffragette City,"
"Jean Genie," "Diamond Dogs," "Rebel Rebel," "Young Americans," "Fame," and
"Golden Years," plus the unreleased, "John I'm Only Dancing."

RCA Records

6
PICTURE
THIS

The main approach into the town centre consisted of a derelict promenade of condemned Victorian houses favoured only by vandals, vagrants and fly-posting crews.
Nina Antonia, *The Prettiest Star* (SAF, London, 2005)

As he passed a passage at the side of the theatre, the kind sixties bands had glowered down on the sleeve of their early albums, a movement caught his eye. A girl was plastering posters along the wall. Just a face and a name. Hers, he presumed.
Susan Hill, *Breaking Glass* (Star, London, 1980)

Travel back to the childhood bedroom of most Blitz habitués and you'd find a David Bowie poster on the wall.
Steve Strange, *Blitzed!* (Orion, London, 2002)

In 1840 Prince Napoleon, the nephew of Bonaparte, decided that the time was ripe for him to claim his birthright and assume control of France. He was at the time in exile in England and, having gathered a few dozen followers about him, he sailed from Gravesend to Boulogne, seemingly convinced that he could win over the town and, replicating his uncle's return from Elba, sweep through the country on a wave of popular support into Paris itself. As it turned out he was promptly arrested and sentenced to life imprisonment (though he subsequently escaped and eventually – disastrously – became Emperor Napoleon III).

So confident had he been in the success of his enterprise, however, that his arsenal for the trip consisted of little more than a batch of posters to be pasted up around Boulogne and points beyond, proclaiming his restoration of the Napoleonic dynasty. And, since crossings of the English Channel were even more unpredictable then than they are now, and he couldn't guarantee the date of the attempted coup, he had left a space at the bottom of the printed text for the date of the proclamation to be completed by hand. It was, in effect, the first tour poster, with a blank strip for the date and venue to be filled in later.

At this stage in the mid-nineteenth century, the putting up of posters was entirely unregulated. Businesses, theatre companies or individuals who had a message they wanted to see displayed went to one of the professional bill-posters who would paste them up wherever he could. As the trade increased, so too did the competition for the best sites, with disputes settled as often as not by physical violence. In the early 1860s Edward Sheldon, who had taken over a bill-posting business in Leeds from his father-in-law, was so badly beaten in a fight with his rivals, Wood & Holdsworth, over a particular site that, fearing he might actually lose his life in a future conflict, he hit upon a radical idea: he rented the wall from its owner and thereby gained the exclusive right to put posters upon it.

Above

The Plasmatics – Live (1980)
The Plasmatics were a New York concept punk band who acquired a reputation for controversy, largely through a set of explosive stage stunts, but who attracted most attention for their singer, former adult-movie actress Wendy O Williams (1949–98). Following a minor British hit with 'Butcher Baby', they were scheduled to make their London debut at the Hammersmith Odeon, but were banned by the Greater London Council – run at the time by the Conservative Party under bow-tie-wearing Sir Horace Cutler – on the grounds that Williams was 'an anarchist'. A British audience was thus denied the opportunity to see her smash up a car (a shame for those who had missed the Move destroy a 1956 Chevy back in the '60s). This poster celebrates the ban.

20 x 30 inches, 76 x 50.5cm

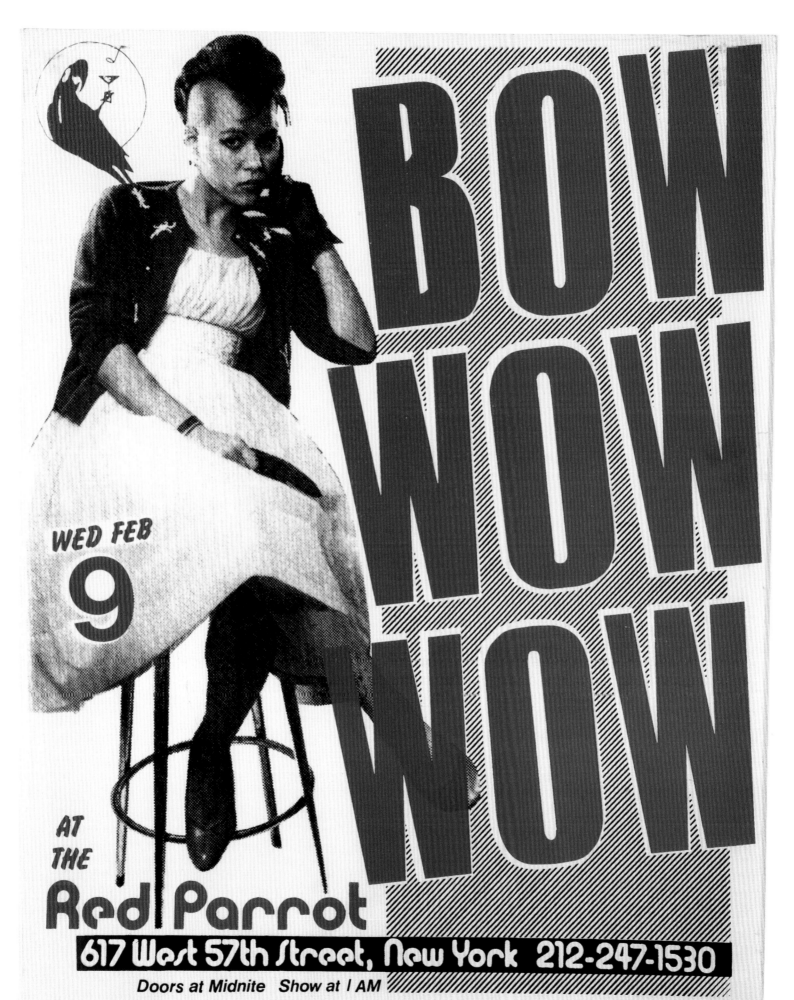

BOW WOW WOW

WED FEB **9**

AT THE **Red Parrot**

617 West 57th Street, New York 212-247-1530

Doors at Midnite   Show at I AM

Tickets $12   Tickets at Ticketron, Sweet B at Fiorucci, Bleecker Bobs, Igor Records.

Thus began the division between paid-for sites and fly-posting, the practice of putting up posters on sites that hadn't been authorized, an activity that was always of dubious legality at best. By 1877 it was estimated that there were around 200 men working legitimately as bill-posters in London, together with a larger – though unquantifiable – number of fly-posters.

The violence did not stop, though the scale of the problem in Britain seldom reached the levels of New York, where street brawls were commonplace in the early years of the twentieth century: 'Police were informed that sixty bill-posters, representing every theatre in town, were fighting for possession of the facades of 104 and 106 West Thirty-Fourth Street,' read one report, adding that the combatants had 'hit one another with mucilage mops and beaten tattoos on heads with handles.' The trade became – and remained – a minor branch of gangsterism; as Joe Boyd discovered when he wanted to advertise the UFO Club, you had to go to one of the hoods who ran fly-posting if you wanted a street presence.

In the rock era, as posters became an essential form of advertising, a covert relationship developed between respectable, multinational record companies and those who operated on the fringes of the criminal underworld. Billboard advertising was very expensive and the alternative, of paying someone to put your stuff up on vacant shops, hoardings and uninhabited houses, was clearly the cheaper option. Rates were negotiated – it was reckoned to cost £30 per hundred posters in 1977, rising to one pound per poster twenty-five years later – and payment, though preferred in cash, could be made by cheque; invoices were also issued, despite the illegality of the enterprise.

Talk of fly-posting in the '70s and '80s is dominated by the mention in hushed tones of such shadowy characters as Terry the Pill. These were the people reputed to control the fly-posting sites in London and beyond, and to look with grave displeasure at anyone who strayed onto their patches, or posted over the work done by their boys. Putting up posters without permission was illegal, but for the amateur who wanted to advertise a gig, it was not the threat of the police that caused concern, so much as fear of the professional villains: even if apprehended and taken to court, the worst that would happen was a small fine, which counted as nothing compared to the stories of retribution meted out by the gangsters who were believed to have first claim on the walls. Many of these tales were undoubtedly apocryphal, but the reputation was sufficient to maintain authority, particularly since, of the many who knew the name of Terry the Pill, very few ever met him. One who did remembers him as 'a real character, something of an eccentric wandering around in a smoking jacket; he sounded a bit like a gangster but he was never threatening in any way. Not to me, anyway.'

So integrated had this side of the business become by the late '70s that the major record companies would send artwork to printing plants with instructions to deliver the posters 'direct to Terry'. For smaller labels the procedure was more colourful; one new employee at a leading independent record company in the early-1980s found that amongst his first tasks was to drive a vanload of posters

Previous page - left
The B52s - *The B52s* (1979)
Originating in Athens, Georgia, the b52s made their name playing at Max's Kansas City and CBGBs. Offering an alternate take on the retro chic of previous bands – from Roxy Music to the Rezillos – they adopted the look of space age suburbia, dreaming of a future that never happened.

Photography George DuBose, art direction Sue AB Surd (Warner Bros) 20 x 30 inches, 76 x 50.5cm

Previous page - right
Bow Wow Wow - Live (1983)
Formed by Malcolm McLaren from the Ants (without Adam) and fronted by singer Annabella Lwin, Bow Wow Wow's early career sometimes seemed like a collection of stunts. But the single of 'I Want Candy' was a big favourite in the early days of MTV and the band acquired a cult following in the USA.

19 x 25 inches, 63.5 x 48cm

Right
The Boys Next Door – *Door Door* (1979)
The only album by Australian band the Boys Next Door, later to metamorphose into the Birthday Party, was promoted by a poster designed by singer Nick Cave. He had studied painting for two years at the Caulfield Institute of Technology in Melbourne, and continued to contribute to the group's artwork, principally with paintings of primitive religious iconography.

Design Nick Cave; 17 x 22 inches, 56 x 43cm

OOVIES

Left

The Flamin' Groovies – UK tour (1978)
The Flamin' Groovies managed to be present at
two musical revolutions and fail commercially
both times. In the late-'60s their hard-driving rock
& roll was out of place in their psychedelia-
drenched hometown of San Francisco; in 1976
they were reclaimed by British punk as
forerunners of the movement, and headlined the
gig that saw the Ramones make their UK debut.
By that time, however, they'd adopted a retro-
powerpop look and sound that was still out of
place.

Their career was also compounded by bad luck
and bad planning. Kris Needs, writing in *ZigZag* of
their 1978 tour supported by Australian band
Radio Birdman, described a gig in Birmingham: 'It
was unfortunate that night the Darts and John
Otway were both up the road (in different venues)
splitting a potential crowd of three or four
thousand between them, leaving the Groovies
with a couple of hundred. I didn't see one poster.'

This poster for the tour was a beautiful piece
of work, but a painting in pastel shades doesn't
really do justice to a band that, Needs claimed,
'must frighten even themselves such is the
incredible POWER they're putting out. A sound
like there's NEVER BEEN before in rock & roll.'

18 x 28 inches, 71 x 46cm

to an underground car park in Kilburn, North London late at night. 'I got out the van and a little old man in brown overalls appeared. He put all the posters in a shopping trolley, and scuttled off with it, up the tunnel that led out of the car park.' On another occasion he was sent to a Red Star office with parcels of posters to be sent express delivery to various villains in the north, including the one who was said to run the walls of Manchester, Leeds and Newcastle.

No money changed hands on either occasion – such transactions being dealt with elsewhere in a shadow economy – but the furtive nature of the enterprise did leave record companies at the mercy of their unofficial business partners. Boyd had reckoned that only half the posters he printed actually got put on walls, and that proportion became accepted as the norm, a regrettable but tolerable level of wastage. Some in the industry even suspected that there was a lucrative side-business in selling off posters for pulping. And just as workers in a pressing-plant were able temporarily to halt the production of the Sex Pistols' single 'God Save the Queen' in protest at its lyrics, so too did an unofficial censorship develop in fly-posting. For the 1974 general election, the Edgar Broughton Band produced a poster featuring a drawing by Ralph Steadman which showed a pair of human buttocks, one cheek of which was the face of Harold Wilson, the other Ted Heath, with a speech bubble emerging from between: 'Why Vote? It's A Double Cross!' It bore the name of the Edgar Broughton Foundation, but advertised nothing other than a distrust of politicians. As their manager, Peter Jenner, remembers, however, the gangsters who controlled the walls turned it down: 'I couldn't put them up anywhere. The word came back they wouldn't handle it because it would give them too much grief.'

For the major record companies there were added benefits: fly-posting conferred a certain street cachet, or at least the illusion of it, and, while it might be cheap compared with using official paid-for sites, it was still too pricey for many of their smaller would-be competitors, as Michael Beal recalls: 'It was hard to get into that scene. The first Hot Rods poster wasn't used for fly-posting 'cos that meant the company paying whoever it was that did London at that time. And that took marketing clout.'

The alternative was to use casual, unaccountable labour, as one opportunist found in 1977; walking into the offices of a major record company, he offered to do some fly-posting for them and was given 200 posters for their latest single and £10 to cover both his work and the purchase of brush and paste. He got a cab home with the money and held on to the posters; nearly three decades later he was selling them on the Internet.

Occasionally a record company would use paid-for sites – a billboard poster for Bowie, announcing that 1976 was his 'golden year', advertised the album *Station To Station*, the movie *The Man Who Fell To Earth* and the forthcoming gigs at the Empire Pool Wembley – but such campaigns were very rare exceptions. In America, however, where the landscape was shaped far more overtly by the demands of the car, and where billboards were therefore of greater interest than

Left
Elvis Costello – *Armed Forces* (1978)
Costello's third album came with a painting of elephants on the cover, which folded out into one of the most exciting pop art sleeves of all time. The poster echoed the wildlife theme (referencing also Peter Beard's photos of dead game) and illustrated the withdrawal from immediate rock & roll imagery.

Design Barney Bubbles (Radar Records) 20 x 30 inches, 76 x 50.5cm

a small-scale fly-poster at street level, the same relationship between major record labels and illegal postering didn't develop. The 1974 campaign for would-be glam star Jobriath was mocked for its self-indulgence ('I'm going to produce the biggest hype you've ever seen,' announced his manager, Jerry Brandt, and got Elektra to pay for a fifty square foot billboard in Times Square), but the principle wasn't as far removed from normality as it would have been in Britain, and primarily it was the hubris of trying this with an unknown act that attracted scorn. The only equivalent in Britain was when Bowie hired a neon display in Piccadilly Circus in January 1974 to wish his fans a happy new year; but then he was at the time the biggest rock star in the country.

THURSDAY 13 NOV. 8.00. MAIN HALL
£1.70 ADV. £2.00 DOOR
STRAY CATS

The Cramps – Live

Despite the band's professed intentions (singer Lux Interior in 1981: 'I don't wanna be elitist, or a cult band, I wanna be a cross between Creedence Clearwater and the Beatles') the Cramps were one of the key cult groups of the early -'80s. Typically of their posters, this was a one-colour screen print onto fluorescent paper, a material that was notoriously difficult to paste up, ensuring that plenty of copies were available to buy at the gigs. The four-sheet size (40 x 60 inches) was the standard for gig posters of the period.

40 x 60 inches, 152.5 x 101.5cm

The Stray Cats – Live (1980)

'The Stray Cats had been on the cover of the *NME* and I expected the venue to be packed,' remembers one of the audience at this Hull University gig. 'Unfortunately, the University didn't advertise outside of the campus and students don't like rockabilly so the audience comprised of about fifteen teddy boy dockers from Hull who'd heard about the gig from a different source.' The support band were Seventeen, later to become the Alarm. A similar drawing of the Statue of Liberty had appeared on the cover of the first issue of *Granta* magazine (an issue titled 'New American Writing').

(Hull University) 16.9 x 24 inches, 60.5 x 43cm

The Soft Boys – 'Give it to the Soft Boys' (1977)
The Soft Boys, fronted by art-school dropout Robyn Hitchcock, were to become one of the great British cult legends, but their debut release failed to make much impact at the time. Perhaps, on balance, the summer of punk wasn't the ideal time to put out the first psychedelic record in ten years. The cuttings from various music papers of the time include adverts and reviews for Slaughter & the Dogs, Barbara Dickson and the Dwight Twilley Band.

Graphics David Jeffry (Raw Records) 12.5 x 17 inches, 43 x 32cm

In general the walls of, say, the seedier districts of New York were considered fair game for amateurs. The first issue of *Punk* magazine was advertised with a poster that declared 'Punk Is Coming' because, as John Holmstrom explains: 'Sniping (fly-posting) was a very popular way to publicize things in the 1970s. There was a lot of empty wall space, and the police weren't aggressively arresting people for postering.' Here, even more than in London, the urban scene was set by fly-postered walls that resembled a trash version of a Warhol gallery exhibition.

Susan Seidelman, who went on to direct Madonna in *Desperately Seeking Susan* as well as the pilot for the TV series *Sex and the City*, made her directorial debut with *Smithereens* (1982), in which Wren, a girl from out of town played by Susan Berman, arrives in New York, gets a job at a photocopying shop and proceeds to plaster the walls of the city with Warholian repeats of her own image. 'What interested me as a filmmaker were the rows of repeating images,' says Seidelman. 'Because the fly posters were made cheaply and often with a Xerox machine, the bands couldn't afford big, slick-looking posters (nor did they want them), so they stuck up long rows of smaller repeating images. The other striking thing was that the same walls were being used over and over again, so that new posters were stuck on top of old posters, creating a kind of collage effect, especially as parts of the old posters were worn off (or ripped off) to make way for the new. The walls themselves became collaborative works of art.'

Such artistic exploitation of the urban landscape was not to last. In 1982 James Q Wilson and George Kelling wrote their influential article 'Broken Windows' in the venerable New England journal *Atlantic Monthly*, arguing that the acceptance of low-level but visible anti-social behaviour adversely affected community confidence, and thereby permitted an escalation in more serious crime. Kelling was subsequently employed as a consultant by the NYC Transit

The Psychedelic Furs –'We Love You' (1979)
Asked about his time at art school, Psychedelic Furs singer Richard Butler commented: 'I was very interested in Andy Warhol, and I ended up doing silk-screen prints a lot of the time.' The influence can be seen in the painting of a radio he did for the sleeve of the band's single 'We Love You', which is the basis of this gig poster. Early copies were silk-screened.

Artwork Richard Butler (CBS Records)
20 x 30 inches, 76 x 50.5cm

THE PSYCHEDELIC FURS ARE BEAUTIFUL CHAOS

'WE LOVE YOU'

NEW SINGLE ON EPIC
RELEASED NOV. 2
THE PSYCHEDELIC FURS

EPC 8005

Above

The Pop Group – Y (1979)
The sleeve for the Pop Group's debut album was by Malcolm Garrett, and the record contained this poster. Appropriately for a band that mixed dub, funk, punk and Kraut-rock with political anger, the lyrics are printed over a photomontage of atrocities committed around the world, from South-East Asia to Northern Ireland.

The Pop Group (Radarscope Records)
53 x 22.5 inches, 135 x 57cm

Authority in 1984 and implemented a crackdown on graffiti and fare-dodging; with the election of Rudy Giuliani as Mayor of New York ten years later, broken window theory resulted in what was known as zero-tolerance policing, and fly-posting became a serious political issue. A comparable process was to happen in Britain in the early twenty-first century, as local authorities sought to eradicate the terrible menace of people putting pieces of paper on walls.

As the 1980s dawned, the threat of punk had been effectively seen off, the harsher, more threatening elements smothered by silence, the softer, more malleable elements slipping into the mainstream.

What was left was a perplexing plethora of revivals. The rock & roll revival that had kicked off the '70s was still going strong, though it had by now been thoroughly assimilated into the entertainment industry: 1978 alone saw the release of the movies *Grease*, *American Hot Wax* and *The Buddy Holly Story*. In the same year Showaddywaddy had three

top 5 hits in the UK; the only glam-era pop band still scoring, they fitted perfectly and harmlessly into the *Summertime Special* end of TV variety. Similarly 1977 saw the start of a four-year run for the American TV series centred on Sha Na Na, veterans of both Woodstock and *Grease*. Elsewhere the movies gave us ersatz psychedelia and mod in the shape of *Sgt Pepper's Lonely Hearts Club Band* (1978) and *Quadrophenia* (1979), and British TV revisited the old formats of *Juke Box Jury* and *Oh Boy* in the last year of the decade.

Above and above - right

David Bowie – *Lodger* (1978)

The sleeve for the album showed Bowie in his most unglamorous pose yet, a collapsed, brutalized figure superimposed on a lavatory wall. The photo session ended early when Bowie pronounced himself satisfied with the preparatory Polaroid shots, so that the quality of the reproduction was reduced, giving the impression of a scene-of-crime snap, and the landscape shape ensured that only his legs were on the front of the sleeve.

The US poster for the record avoided these downbeat associations, by placing colourful images behind the picture of Bowie, giving an inappropriately aspirational tone to the piece. The European version, however, made the image even more grubby with the inclusion of a string-vest.

Photography Brian Duffy (RCA Records & Tapes)
Above
16.5 x 22 inches, 56.5 x 41cm
Above - right
23 x 35 inches, 89 x 58.5cm

In musical terms, the resurgence of rock & roll, pioneered in Britain by Shakin' Stevens & the Sunsets and Crazy Cavan & the Rhythm Rockers, had been augmented by the unexpected return of rockabilly that brought a more youthful wave of bands (Flying Saucers, Whirlwind). There was also, to name only the most prominent practitioners, a rebirth of interest in mod (Secret Affair, Chords), ska (the Specials, Madness), doo-wop (Rocky Sharpe & the Razors, Darts), heavy metal (Iron Maiden, Saxon), psychedelia (Soft Boys, Barracudas) and r&b (Inmates, Red Beans & Rice). And then there was Thamesbeat – a short-lived London version of Merseybeat, centred on the Pleasers – and indeed punk itself, regurgitated in a series of ever more desperate guises championed by *Sounds* magazine, including Oi and Pathetic Punk. There was even the hint of a glam revival with Joan Jett's massive international hit 'I Love Rock & Roll' (originally written and recorded by Arrows), with Gary Glitter reinventing himself as a live attraction, and with Slade – on the verge of splitting up – proving to be the unexpected hit of the 1980 Reading Festival. (Curiously enough, the arch-punk John Lydon seemed to endorse much of this revivalism, turning up at gigs by Darts and Gary Glitter and, in 1977, enthusing about Shakin' Stevens: 'Fucking good singer,' he pointed out.)

Symbolic of this dispersal of the tribes, the charts pages in *Sounds* had by 1981 expanded from being simply the top fifty singles and albums in the UK and US to include such categories as Video, Alternative, Heavy Metal, Oi, Imports, Disco, Futurist, Rockabilly, Reggae (pre-release, singles and albums), Euro Rock and Jap

Techno Rock. This was, according to one's point of view, either the splendid flowering of a thousand blooms or a last desperate attempt to find a standard around which youth could rally, a search for consensus in the face of social upheaval. In either event it did suggest the end of a boom generation, weighed down with nostalgia, an impression confirmed by the first ever auction of rock memorabilia at Sotheby's in 1980.

And one other fact was inescapable: the decline in record sales. In their annual figures at the end of June 1979, EMI Records revealed that they'd turned in a profit of just £1.9m on sales of £166m; worse than that, the second half of the period showed a loss of £14.6m. In isolation EMI might have been considered a special case, a company trading on past glories (in 1973 more than a quarter of its profits had been accounted for by the sales of the two Beatles double-album compilations), but unfortunately it wasn't an isolated case: record sales generally were down year-on-year by 30 per cent in the UK and by 50 per cent in the US.

A contributory factor in this decline of the industry was the siphoning off of creative talent into what became the indie music scene. The punk ethos of not selling out to the rock industry had been more trumpeted than observed with the original wave of bands, but it became a respectable position to adopt as the '80s arrived, and bands like the Fire Engines and the Fall – however influential they were to be – refused to play by the rules demanded of would-be pop stars. Adam Ant's acceptance of the art of selling was, as he acknowledges, not universal: 'It's part of the work, it's part of the job. But there were a lot of people on the other side of things, the industrial bands and so on, rejecting that.'

Instead there was a return to the more elliptical imagery that had characterized the prog-rock era. There was little about the sleeves of, say, Joy Division's two albums to indicate the contents: stylish, intriguing and obscure, Peter Saville's design for the cover of *Unknown Pleasures* (1979) would have been equally fitting for Pink Floyd's *Dark Side of the Moon*. The same year the Gang of Four's debut album, *Entertainment!*, came in a sleeve designed by guitarist Andy Gill – a fine arts graduate from Leeds University – that would have looked perfectly at home in a gallery, but again revealed nothing about the music.

David Bowie - 'Ashes to Ashes' *Scary Monsters*
(1980)
Right
David Bowie – *Scary Monsters* (1980)
Edward Bell studied at the Royal College of Art
and became a photographer before moving into
painting. His first exhibition was staged in a
Covent Garden gallery in 1980 and was attended
by David Bowie, who was sufficiently impressed
to ask Bell to design his next album sleeve, which
was needed within a week.

Bowie already had a photo session arranged
with Brian Duffy, after which Bell took a set of
shots: 'The first thing I did was get him to take
the hat off.' He also encouraged his subject to
smear his lipstick in pursuit of a more decadent
image of Pierrot. The resulting painting bore the
influence of Warhol (as seen on his sleeve for the
Rolling Stones' *Love You Live*) and Richard
Hamilton. Both Duffy's and Bell's images were
used in the publicity campaign for the album and
its lead single 'Ashes to Ashes'.

Bell also painted a picture for himself from the
same source material, which he titled 'Glamour'.
Bowie saw it hanging in his home and asked if he
could buy it. It was subsequently turned into a
poster by the leading commercial firm Pace
Minerva.

178

Previous page
Photography Brian Duffy; painting Edward Bell
(RCA Records & Tapes) 15 x 27 inches, 68.5 x 38cm
Right
Painting & design Edward Bell (RCA Records &
Tapes) 24 x 48 inches, 122 x 61cm

In the immediate future, though, it was Adam Ant who was showing the way forward, recognizing two key trends in the marketing of pop that were the shape of things to come. The first was the collapse of the weekly music press. The years 1980–83 saw the sales of the four surviving weeklies (*NME*, *Melody Maker*, *Record Mirror*, *Sounds*) fall by nearly 50 per cent; during the same period, however, there was a 35 per cent increase in sales of music magazines overall, with the difference accounted for by fledgling titles *Smash Hits*, *The Face* and *Number 1*. This new breed of publication was in full colour, printed on glossy paper rather than the newsprint of the existing titles, and issued fortnightly or monthly; it paid more attention to image and style, and consequently less to the music itself. The heyday of the weeklies was over, their decline hastened by an ever more desperate chase of indie white rabbits down ever more unreal rabbit holes. By the end of the century there would be just one title left, the *NME*, to celebrate new bands, many of whom, ironically, were now turning for inspiration to that very post-punk period that had ended the dominance of the weekly papers.

The second key factor in the dawning of a new era was the massive growth in promotional videos. 'At art school I'd learnt to storyboard short films,' remembers Adam, 'so when the video thing came around, I was there. I could storyboard it with no interference and give it to Mike Mansfield, who'd started making TV pop films with Billy Fury, and he made people look glamorous.'

And, despite the revivals, the indie sector and the overcoat-clad electro-industrial bands, it was glamour that was to be the next big thing of the early '80s. Just as British punk had been created by a generation of glam fans brought up on *Ziggy Stardust* and *Diamond Dogs*, so the new romantics who came out of the London club scene initiated by Steve Strange and Rusty Egan were also glam fans, but with the crucial difference of a couple of years in age; in this context, the adoption of dance music by Bowie and Roxy Music in the mid-'70s was more significant than their earlier art-rock incarnations. The beat had changed, but the celebration of stardom and posing remained. So too did the playing with gender identity, as Trevor Bolder of the Spiders From Mars reflects: 'Punk destroyed a lot of music. It came in and cleaned everything out. It came in with a bang and fizzled out at the end, I thought, and then everyone went back to wearing bloody make-up again.'

And in this world, the video was self-evidently a more efficient way of selling an act's image than the static poster could ever be. Commercial posters remained, of course, since fans still wished to adorn their bedroom walls – indeed they were being printed in ever larger numbers under ever more professional contracts – but they had become part of a larger machine, and were seen as commodities in their own right, with the most successful bands releasing new pieces on a monthly basis. Similarly fly-posting was also becoming a less haphazard business, with record companies experimenting with images printed across more than one sheet, typically two double-crown size (30"x 40") posters that formed a single advert, to reinforce a publicity campaign for a new release. The gap between fly-posting and billboards narrowed, though in a more crowded environment, the significance of posters was simultaneously diminished: their role now was in support of video campaigns.

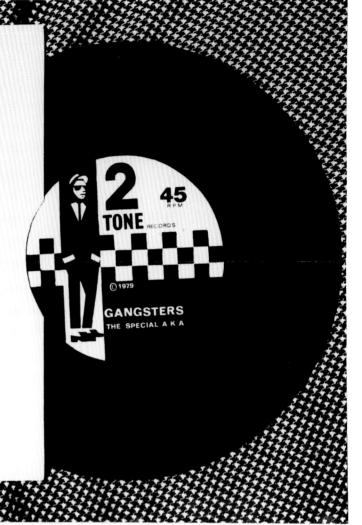

THE SPECIAL A.K.A.
GANGSTERS

VS.
THE SELECTER

David Bowie, astute enough to exploit a fashion before anyone quite realized it was fashionable, was amongst the first to explore the possibilities of video, producing a series of classic promo films that began with 'Boys Keep Swinging' (1979). Admittedly his drag routine in that was sufficiently disturbing that, when it was aired on *Top of the Pops*, the single promptly dropped down the charts, but it was immediately identifiable as a classic piece of imagery: *Record Mirror*, eagerly tailing the new trend, produced a centrefold poster based on shots from the film. Even more influential was the video for 'Ashes to Ashes' (1980), in which he appeared in full-on Pierrot outfit, heralding the return of 'bloody make-up'.

In August 1981 MTV began broadcasting in America, and the art-school tradition of British rock, which had ensured that video was taken seriously as a medium, meant that it was UK acts who reaped the immediate benefits: it was Bowie's

The Special AKA – 'Gangsters' (1979)
The first single on the 2-Tone record label featured two new bands: the group later to be known as the Specials and, on the b-side, the Selector. The poster, illustrating the 7-inch single being taken out of its sleeve, has a background of a dog-tooth fabric, echoing the chequerboard pattern of the label's logo. The term 'vs' is derived from dub reggae albums, while the rude boy drawing was by Jerry Dammers, the central figure in both the Specials and 2-Tone.

Design Jerry Dammers (2-Tone) 16 x 24 inches, 60.5 x 41cm

Above - left

Red Beans & Rice – 'That Driving Beat' (19??)
The post-punk fallout saw a revival in Britain of r&b, operating in the space opened by the likes of Dr Feelgood and the Count Bishops. Red Beans & Rice were amongst those working the London pub circuit and released this single on Chiswick Records, the label that had pioneered the indie scene. The poster also drew on the sartorial style of the mod revival.

(Chiswick) 14.75 x 30 inches, 76.5 x 37.5 cm

children, from Marc Almond to Boy George to Duran Duran, that made all the running.

But while the advent of music video was instantly recognizable as a revolutionary force in rock & roll, there was one other development whose impact was slower to make an impact. In 1982 the compact disc was launched by a consortium of record companies led by Philips and Sony. The replacement of the standard 12-inch LP with the 12cm CD was a more gradual process (it took five years for CD sales to outstrip vinyl albums), but it was destined to change forever the nature of sleeve design and therefore of rock artwork. The canvas was so much reduced, by comparison with the LP cover and its accompanying poster, that the album sleeve was destined in the future to play a subsidiary role to the video.

And still further behind the scenes was the music that was, to the surprise of the entire industry, to challenge and overtake rock & roll itself as the cutting edge of popular culture. Hip hop emerged in the '70s in the South Bronx as a seemingly minor sub-genre of disco and initially, perhaps inevitably, made a greater commercial impact in Britain than it did in the States beyond New York City: the Sugarhill Gang's 1979 single 'Rapper's Delight' reached #3 in the UK while struggling to breach

Right
TV Smith's Explorers – 'Tomahawk Cruise' (1980)
The first single by the band TV Smith's Explorers, formed after the Adverts split, was one of the few examples of Ralph Steadman drawing for a rock & roll record.

Artwork & design Ralph Steadman (Epic Records)
30 x 43 inches, 109 x 76.5cm

TV SMITH'S E

PLORERS

se between living and

Tomahawk

ruise

GRACE JONES . . .

"WARM LEATHERETTE"

Left
Grace Jones – 'Warm Leatherette' (1980)
Grace Jones was to become emblematic of the
heavily styled side of the early-'80s represented
by, above all, *The Face* magazine. 'We're all in the
fashion business,' Island boss Chris Blackwell once
commented. 'You used to be able to sell records
purely on music and musicianship. Now it's
packaging, media, television and video.'

Photography & design Jean Paul Goude; clothes
Issey Miyake (Island Records) 23 x 35 inches,
88.5 x 58.5cm

BAUHAUS

the *Billboard* top 40. In a world where rock was still torn between two loves – a revival of anything it could get its hands on and a style-driven generation of vapid, vacuous, video artists – hip hop offered the clearest way forward: a street culture with mass appeal and a potential for intelligence.

In December 1982 Malcolm McLaren, managerial veteran of the New York Dolls, the Sex Pistols and Bow Wow Wow, finally entered the British charts in his own right with the hip hop-derived 'Buffalo Gals'. The posters that promoted the single featured, for the first time, not the artist but a set of twin-deck turntables, making explicit the triumph of disco over rock. The same month, as if in acknowledgement of the passing of the baton, Max's Kansas City, the New York club that Andy Warhol had described as the 'spot where Pop Art and Pop Life came together', closed its doors for the last time.

Meanwhile, in South London, a new club had opened that was to be at the heart of the new romantic movement and subsequently of house and acid. The Fridge in Brixton was created by Andrew Czezowski and Susan Carrington, who had run London's leading punk venue, the Roxy, back in 1977, and its launch was announced with full-page adverts in *The Face*. Was it also accompanied by a poster campaign? 'Oh no,' says Carrington. 'Posters were far too rock & roll.'

Above

Bauhaus – *In the Flat Field* (1980)
Three of the four members of the Bauhaus attended Nene Art School in Northampton; the fourth – singer Peter Murphy – had been offered a place but turned it down and became instead a printer's apprentice ('I spent five years printing beer mats and letter heads'). Drawing on both glam and heavy rock, the artistic aspirations of the band were apparent from its name onwards – originally it had been even more specific as Bauhaus 1919.

Photography Duane Michals (4AD) 16.5 x 24 inches, 61 x 42.5cm

Right

Joy Division – 'An Ideal For Living' (1978)
The first Joy Division record was a self-released EP that replaced punk's urban aesthetic with an industrial image that was to point the way forward for a section of early-'80s British rock.

Design Bernard Sumner (Anonymous/Enigma Records) 17 x 24.5 inches, 62 x 43cm

JOY DIVISION

AN IDEAL FOR LIVING — an anonymous records 12" ep

Above and right

Malcolm McLaren – 'Buffalo Gals' (1982)

Acknowledging that rock had lost control of the cutting edge of popular culture to hip hop, the poster for Malcolm McLaren's single 'Buffalo Gals' is perhaps the first use of the twin-deck icon in promotional material. The amateurish photomontage harks back to punk, while the faceless focus on technology echoes the imagery employed at the time by austere electronica acts like Cabaret Voltaire. Following the 'now form a band' message of 1977 punk, the small print tells you how to scratch:

Two manual decks and a rhythm box is all you need. Get a bunch of good rhythm records, choose your favourite part and groove along with the rhythm machine. Using your hands, scratch the records repeating the grooves you dig so much. Fade one record into the other and keep that rhythm box going. Now start talking and singing over the record with your own microphone. Now you're making your own music out of other people's records. That's what scratching is.

Right
(Charisma) 20 x 30 inches, 76 x 50.5cm
Above
(Island/Atco) 40 x 60 inches, 152.5 x 101.5cm

BIBLIOGRAPHY

In addition to back issues of the various music papers of the period (*Melody Maker, NME, Record Mirror, ZigZag, Disc, Sounds, Rolling Stone* and *Punk*), mention must also be made of the historical work of *Mojo* magazine in recent years.

A lifetime of reading about rock & roll means that much information has been gleaned from a now untraceable multitude of sources, but the following books have been of particular value:

Antonia, Nina, *Too Much, Too Soon: The Make-Up and Break-Up of the New York Dolls* (Omnibus, London, 1998)

Antonia, Nina, *The Prettiest Star: Whatever Happened to Brett Smiley* (SAF, London, 2005)

Balfour, Rex, *The Bryan Ferry Story* (Michael Dempsey, London, 1976)

Balls, Richard, *Sex & Dugs & Rock 'n' Roll: The Life of Ian Dury* (Omnibus, London, 2000)

Benn, Tony, *Conflicts of Interest: Diaries 1977–80* (Hutchinson, London, 1990)

Bockris, Victor, *Lou Reed: The Biography* (Hutchinson, London, 1994)

Bockris, Victor, *Patti Smith* (Fourth Estate, London, 1998)

Booth, Stanley, *The True Adventures of the Rolling Stones* (William Heinemann, London, 1985)

Bowman, David, *Fa fa fa fa fa fa: The Adventures of Talking Heads in the 20th Century* (Bloomsbury, London, 2001)

Burgess, Paul & Parker, Alan, *Satellite: Sex Pistols Memorabilia, Locations, Photography, Fashion* (Abstract Sounds Publishing, London, 1999)

Burke, John, *Privilege* (Pan, London, 1967)

Cann Kevin, *David Bowie: A Chronology* (Vermilion, London, 1983)

Clark, Tim (ed.), *The Island Book of Posters* (Island Records, London, 1991)

Connolly, Ray, *Stardust* (Fontana, London, 1974)

County, Jayne with Rupert Smith, *Man Enough to be a Woman* (Serpent's Tail, London, 1995)

Crow, Thomas *The Rise of the Sixties* (Everyman Art Library, London, 1996)

Elliott, Larry & Dan Atkinson, *The Age of Insecurity* (Verso, London, 1998)

Everett, Peter, *You'll Never Be 16 Again: An Illustrated History of the British Teenager* (BBC, London, 1986)

Farren, Mick (ed.), *Get On Down: A Decade of Rock & Roll Posters* (Futura Dempsey & Squires, London, 1976)

Farren, Mick, *The Black Leather Jacket* (Abbeville, New York, 1985)

Frith, Simon, *Sound Effects: Youth, Leisure and the Politics of Rock 'n' Roll* (Pantheon, New York, 1981)

Frith, Simon & Horne, Howard, *Art Into Pop* (Methuen, London, 1987)

Furmanovsky, Jill, *The Moment: 25 Years of Rock Photography* (Paper Tiger, London, 1995)

Garfield, Simon *The Wrestling* (Faber & Faber, London, 1996)

Gilbert, Pat, *Passion is a Fashion: The Real Story of The Clash* (Aurum, London, 2004)

Gillman, Peter & Leni, *Alias David Bowie* (Hodder & Stoughton, London, 1986)

Gimarc, George, *Punk Diary 1970–1979* (Vintage, London, 1994)

Glitter, Gary, *Leader* (Ebury, London, 1991)

Green, Jonathan, *Days In The Life: Voices from the English Underground 1961–1971* (William Heinemann, London, 1988)

Gorman, Clem, *Back Stage Rock: Behind the Scenes with the Bands* (Pan, London, 1978)

Grove, Martin A., *Teen Idols* (Manor, New York, 1979)

Hackett, Pat (ed.), *The Andy Warhol Diaries* (Warner Books, New York, 1989)

Hamilton, Richard, *Collected Works 1963–82* (Thames and Hudson, London, 1982)

Hare, David, *Teeth 'n' Smiles* (Faber & Faber, London, 1976)

Hoskyns, Barney, *Glam: Bowie, Bolan and the Glitter Rock Revolution* (Faber, London, 1998)

Hunter, Ian, *Diary of a Rock 'n' Roll Star* (Panther, London, 1974)

Kent, Nick, *The Dark Stuff* (Penguin, London,1994)

Kirk, Kris & Heath, Ed, *Men In Frocks* (GMP, London, 1984)

Laing, Dave, *One Chord Wonders: Power and Meaning in Punk Rock* (OUP, Milton Keynes, 1985)

Livingstone, Marco, *Pop Art: A Continuing History* (Thames & Hudson, London, 1990)

Logan, Nick & Woffinden, Bob (eds.), *The Illustrated New Musical Express Encyclopaedia of Rock* (Salamander, London, 1977)

McNeil, Legs & McCain, Gillian, *Please Kill Me: The Uncensored Oral History of Punk* (Little, Brown & Co, London, 1996)

Maw, James, *The Official Adam Ant Story* (Futura, London, 1981)

Melly, George, *Revolt Into Style: The Pop Arts in Britain* (Allen Lane, London, 1970)

Moers, Ellen, *The Dandy: Brummell to Beerbohm* (Secker & Warburg, London, 1960)

Nobakht, David, *Suicide: No Compromise* (SAT Publishing, London, 2005)

Novick, Jeremy & Middles, Mick, *Wham Bam Thank You Glam: A Celebration of the '70s* (Aurum, London, 1998)

Rickards, Maurice, *The Rise and Fall of the Poster* (David & Charles, Newton Abbot, 1971)

Rock, Mick, *Raw Power: Iggy and The Stooges 1972* (Creation Books International, London, 2000)

Rock, Mick, *Blood and Glitter: Glam – An Eyewitness Account* (Omnibus, London, 2001)

Rock, Mick, *Moonage Daydream: The Life and Times of Ziggy Stardust* (Genesis, Guildford, 2002)

Rombes, Nicholas, *Ramones* (Continuum, New York, 2005)

Rudd, Natalie, *PB: Peter Blake* (Tate Publishing, London, 2003)

Savage, Jon, *England's Dreaming: Sex Pistols and Punk Rock* (Faber & Faber, London, 1991)

Sewall-Ruskin, Yvonne, *High On Rebellion: Inside the Underground at Max's Kansas City* (Thunder's Mouth Press, New York, 1998)

Sheldon, Cyril, *A History of Poster Advertising* (Chapman & Hall, London, 1937)

Smith, Patti, *Complete: Lyrics, Notes and Reflections* (Bloomsbury, London, 1999)

Thompson, Elizabeth & Gutman, David (ed), *The Bowie Companion* (Macmillan, London, 1993)

Timmers, Margaret (ed.), *The Power of the Poster* (V&A Publications, London, 1998)

Turcotte, Bryan Ray & Miller, Christopher T., *Fucked Up + Photocopied: Instant Art of The Punk Rock Movement* (Gingko Press, Los Angeles, 1999)

Turner, Alwyn W., *Biba: The Biba Experience* (Antique Collectors' Club, Woodbridge, 2004)

Walker, John A., *Crossovers: Art Into Pop/Pop Into Art* (Methuen, London, 1987)

Waugh, Auberon, *A Bed of Flowers* (Michael Joseph, London, 1972)

Weird & Gilly, *Mick Ronson: The Spider with the Platinum Hair* (Independent Music Press, London, 2003)

Wilcken, Hugo, *Low* (Continuum, New York, 2005)

PICTURE CREDITS

The photographs for this book were taken by Fernando Mañoso-Borgas, except for those which were taken by Jon Meade (pages 20, 40, 42, 72, 82, 110, 111, 112, 137, 148 and 151). Our gratitude to both.

We would like to thank the following for lending us posters for this project:

Adam Ant (pp. 114–15), Greg Vandike (p. 117), Martyn Goddard (pp. 95, 144 and 146), Martyn Turner (p.174), Robin Coates (p. 65), Spizz (pp. 113 and 140), TV Smith (pp. 96, 98, 152 and 182) and Thamasin Marsh (p.20).

The poster on p. 33 is © John Pasche.

The poster on pp. 182–3 is © Ralph Steadman.

BEDROOM WALL PHOTOS

Chapter 1 (clockwise from top left):
Marc Bolan, photography Tony Russell (Unique Art Poster, 1972); David Bowie, photography Aaron Sixx (Pace International Ltd, 1972); Mick Jagger, photography Raffaelli, graphic design Jim Robertson (The Visual Thing Inc, 1969); Marc Bolan, photography Stuart Richmond (Poster Verkerke Reprodukties BV); Marc Bolan, photography Tony Russell (Unique Art Poster, 1972); David Bowie, free poster with the LP *The Man Who Sold The World* (RCA Records & Tapes, 1972); David Bowie, free poster with the LP *Space Oddity* (RCA Records & Tapes, 1972); Mott the Hoople, advert for *Brain Capers* from *Melody Maker*, 1971; Lou Reed, advert for *Lou Reed*, 1972; Marc Bolan, photography Keith Morris (Q Posters, 1972); Marc Bolan, photography Richard Fitzgerald (Big O Posters Ltd); Marc Bolan, (Splash Posters Ltd); Marc Bolan, photography Keith Morris (Q Posters, 1972); Mick & Keith, photography Gijsbert Hankeroot (Unique Art Poster, 1972)

Chapter 2 (clockwise from top left):
David Bowie (Splash Posters Ltd) David Bowie; Marc Bolan; David Bowie, photography Robert Failla (Great Western Distributors Inc); David Bowie, photography Mick Rock (Rex Features Ltd); Ron & Russell Mael, photo courtesy of Granada TV's 45 (*Jackie* centrefold, 1974); Mick Ronson, photography Leee Black Childers (Mick Ronson Fan Club); Mick Jagger (*Sounds* centrefold, 1973); *New York Dolls*, advert for New York Dolls, 1973; Iggy and the Stooges, advert for *Raw Power* from *Rolling Stone*, photography Mick Rock,1973; Suzi Quatro (*Intro* magazine); Suzi Quatro (Sousikki aina ajan hermolla); David Bowie (*Popfoto* magazine); David Bowie, concept by House of Ideas (Eurodecor, 1974) David Bowie, Henry Denials Talent Trust (Pace Minerva)

Chapter 3 (clockwise from top left):
Sex Pistols, 'Pretty Vacant' promotion, artwork Jamie Reid (Virgin Records, 1977); Johnny Rotten, photography Ray Stevenson (Rex Features Ltd, 1977); David Bowie (Pace International, 1976); Sex Pistols, photography Dennis Morris; Johnny Rotten; Eddie and the Hot Rods (*Blue Jeans* centrefold); Iggy and the Stooges, *Metallic KO* (Skydog Records); Richard Hell (photo from *ZigZag* magazine); Iggy and the Stooges, advert for *Raw Power* from *Rolling Stone*, photography Mick Rock,1973; David Bowie, "*Heroes*" promotion (RCA Records & Tapes, 1977); Lou Reed (*Popster* magazine no. 17); Television, *Marquee Moon* promotion (Elektra Records, 1977); Richard Hell and the Voidoids, 'The Blank Generation'; The Damned (Stiff Records, 1976)

Chapter 4 (clockwise from top left):
Adverts, *Crossing the Red Sea* promotion (1978); Sex Pistols; Adverts, 'Gary Gilmore's Eyes' promotion, design Nick De Ville (1978); Ian Dury, *New Boots and Panties* promotion (Stiff Records, 1978); Blondie, Parallel Lines promotion (Chrysalis Records, 1978); The Clash, *Give 'Em Enough Rope* promotion (CBS, 1978); Iggy Pop, *TV Eye Live* promotion (RCA Records & Tapes, 1978); Iggy Pop and James Williamson, *Kill City* promotion (Bomp Records, 1977); Debbie Harry, photography Robert Ellis (Big O Posters, 1978); Gaye Advert, photography London Features International (Big O Posters, 1978); David Bowie, *Stage* promotion (RCA Records & Tapes, 1978); David Bowie (*Rock Superstars* poster magazine no.2, 1975); Iggy Pop, tour programme/poster (1978); Siouxsie and the Banshees/Spizzoil/Human League live (1978)

Chapter 5 (clockwise from top left):
David Bowie, *Lodger* promotion, photography Duffy (RCA Records & Tapes, 1978); Adam of the Ants (Pace Minerva, 1980); Ian Dury (Pace International); Iggy Pop, German tour poster (F. Bahruth, 1979); David Bowie (Scandecor, 1976); David Bowie (*Record Mirror* centrefold); the B52's, album promotion (Island Records, 1979); Blondie, 'Heart of Glass' promotion (Chrysalis Records, 1979); Patti Smith (Pace International); Adam and the Ants (Personality Posters UK Ltd); Generation X (Pace International, 1979); Patti Smith; Devo (Pace International, 1979); Blondie, 'Atomic' promotion (Chrysalis Records, 1980)

Chapter 6 (clockwise from top left):
Brian Eno, reissued albums promotion (EG Records Ltd, 1981); Motorhead, *Ace of Spades* promotion (Bronze Records, 1980); Animal Records promotion (Animal); the Cramps, *Songs The Lord Taught Us* promotion (Illegal Records, 1980); the Clash, photography London Features International (Eurodecor, 1981); Edie Sedgwick and Andy Warhol film season, design Neville Brody (Scala Cinema, London); Debbie Harry; David Bowie, *changesonebowie* promotion (RCA Records & Tapes, 1976); James Brown, Jacques Combet IPH/Photo X (Polydor)

The chapter titles come from songs by Eno, Mott the Hoople, David Bowie, X-Ray Spex, Alternative TV and Blondie.

AUTHORS' ACKNOWLEDGEMENTS

Primarily we have to thank those people who were kind enough to share their memories and insights with us:

Adam Ant, Alice Cooper, Andrew Czezowski, Andy Ayers, Andy Shernoff, Angie Bowie, Barrie Masters, Barry Jones, Bob Fisher, Bruce Carleton, Cliff Richards, Dave Hill, Edward Bell, George Underwood, Jamie Reid, Jayne County, Jill Furmanovsky, Jimi LaLumia, Joe Boyd, Joe Petagno, John Holmstrom, John Pasche, John Springate, Kate Simon, Karl Stoecker, Kenny Vaher, Marco Pirroni, Martin Powderly, Martin J Walker, Martyn Goddard, Michael Beal, Mike Gibson, Nigel Weymouth, Nikki Sudden, Nina Antonia, Patti Palladin, Pete Jenner, Poly Styrene, Ray Dorset, Ray Stevenson, Richard Hell, Roberta Bayley, Rodney Bingenheimer, Russell Mael, Spizz, Steve Thomas, Susan Carrington, Susan Seidelman, Suzi Quatro, Tam Paton, Tom Robinson, Tony Linkin, Trevor Bolder and TV Smith.

Also those who provided further information and contacts, or who lent us posters: Adia Wright, Angela Finbow, Aquarium Gallery, Arterie Gallery, Cosham Decor, Elizabeth Hahn, Flowers Gallery, Franklin Marsh, Glyn Brown, Greg Vandike, Jake Shillingford, Madeline Bocchiaro, Mal Campbell, Mark Eastment, Mark Ellicot, Maureen Silverman, Michael Nutley, Michaela Freeman, Michele Kirsch, Michelle Coomber, Paul Tunkin, Robin Coates, Rock Archive, Rose Nag, Ruth Widén, Simon Bowley, Simon Henwood, Steve Doak, Steven Lowe, Stephen Maycock and Sue Harris.

Special thanks to our agent Michael O'Connor, to our editor Natasha Martin, to copy-editor Jon Butler, to Graham Coster, Graham Eames, Lizzie Curtin and Phoebe Clapham at Aurum, and to Chris Shamwana at Ghost. Also to Stephen Bateman and the Partners at Pentagram, and to Sheppard Robson Architects for their understanding.

Even more special thanks to Maria Evagora and Thamasin Marsh.

This book was conceived in John's Café and born in Café Moretti. We note the passing of both with sadness.